DISASTER AT JOHNSTOWN
The Great Flood

"Run for your lives—the dam is breaking!" was a familiar threat to the people of Johnstown, Pennsylvania. They had heard it too often to believe it would ever happen. But on May 31, 1889, disaster roared down from the hills, engulfing the peaceful valley. Thousands of men, women, and children fought with heroic courage to survive through days and nights of horror.

In this vivid, hour-by-hour account, Hildegarde Dolson tells how the tragedy happened, and how such a disaster could have been prevented. It is an exciting story of human bravery.

DISASTER AT JOHNSTOWN
The Great Flood

by HILDEGARDE DOLSON
illustrated by JOSEPH CELLINI

Landmark
BOOKS

RANDOM HOUSE   NEW YORK

ACKNOWLEDGMENTS

I am grateful to the President of the Cambria County Historical Society, Mr. R. F. Pruner, for the loan of books from his private collection and for maps of Johnstown before the flood. My thank-you's also go to John James, executive editor of the Johnstown *Tribune-Democrat*, for the excellent source material in their anniversary flood issue. And, as always, I am deeply grateful to James Stevenson, Dr. Sylvester K. Stevens, and Don Kent of the Pennsylvania Historical and Museum Commission for all their help.

H.D.

Designed by Sallie Baldwin

Library of Congress catalog card number: 64-24811

FOR ALFRED O'TOOLE
with love

CONTENTS

Danger Overhead   *3*

Warning Signs   *12*

Friday Morning in Johnstown   *30*

The Dam Bursts   *48*

The Flood Hits Johnstown   *66*

Day of Courage   *79*

The Night in Alma Hall   *92*

The Fire Rages   *100*

Rescues Down-river   *110*

One Hundred Reporters   *122*

Help Pours In   *142*

Johnstown: Free from Floods   *160*

Bibliography   *167*

Index   *169*

DISASTER AT JOHNSTOWN
The Great Flood

Danger Overhead

All that drizzly Saturday, newsboys in Pittsburgh, the nearest big city, were shouting, "Extra! Extra! . . . Town of Johnstown wiped out. . . . Dam at lake bursts. . . . Floods rush down the valley. . . . Thousands of men, women, children swallowed up. . . . Read all about it. . . . Extra! Extra!"

Eighty miles away, at the foot of Pennsylvania's Allegheny Mountains, dazed, half-naked survivors huddled on the hills, looking down at the oozing mud wreckage of their homes. A boy who had stood there the afternoon before, on that tragic Friday, May 31, 1889, told a reporter how the flood hit after the rotting old dam gave way and sent twenty million tons of water roaring down upon the valley. "It was as if a giant's hand cleared a table, knocking everything off."

Another survivor admitted, "I have often heard it said that the dam might break, but I never paid any attention before." He mentioned that it had been "common talk" every year during the heavy spring rains.

The danger had been there so long that most of

the thirty thousand people in Johnstown and its
nine smaller sister boroughs let the worry roll off
their backs. Anyway, they were used to floods.
Rivers enclosed Johnstown on two sides, and almost
every year when spring rains turned the mountain
streams into boiling torrents, first the Little Conemaugh River and then Stony Creek overflowed.
Cellars of houses along the riverbanks filled up.
Coal floated out of basement bins to make the
dirty water even blacker. Grumbling householders
took up their parlor carpets and moved upstairs
for a day or two. Everyone who lived in the lower
parts of town accepted the annual wetting as a
nuisance that couldn't be helped, like an unwanted
relative coming to visit every year. After all, the
abundance of water power, along with the rich ore
in the hills, had helped to make Johnstown one of
the three great centers in the world for iron and
steel production. The plants and mills belched
black smoke and prosperity over the valley
throughout the year.

All the factories and furnaces were in the outlying boroughs that stretched along the river, with
Johnstown as the main link in the chain. People
came into town to shop, go to the bank, the main
post office, the theater, the opera. Johnstown had
sixteen churches, fourteen hotels, and at least fifty
saloons. It had a population of twelve thousand,
with eighteen thousand more in the sister boroughs.

The day before the flood, Johnstown looked
more bustling than ever. The Reverend Mr.

Chapman, who lived on the park near the center of town, said he had never seen the place so crowded. People from all the outlying boroughs were hurrying across the nine bridges that led into Johnstown. On foot, in buggies, or in horse-drawn street trolleys, they were arriving for the biggest local event of the year, the Memorial Day Parade. In Veterans' Hall, right across the park from Mr. Chapman's Methodist parsonage, the Flower Committee of the Ladies' Relief Corps were arranging wreaths and bouquets for the veterans' graves. They had been hard put to find enough flowers near home, because storms had scattered the blossoms like confetti. Three ladies had driven in a carriage almost to South Fork Dam, twelve miles east of Johnstown, to collect wild columbine, honeysuckle, and piney buds. They had noticed that Buttermilk Falls, usually a clear trickle over rocks, was a churning yellow-brown cascade. In the pine-scented woods, the ground was so soggy that it sucked at their feet like glue.

That spring there had been the heaviest rainfall in the history of the county, 52.67 inches. The day before Memorial Day, the United States Government Signal Service (like our Weather Bureau today) had sent out warnings that new storms were heading east and would strike the Allegheny Mountains and the already sopping-wet Conemaugh Valley. But almost nobody worried about what these storms might do to the already rain-swollen artificial lake enclosed by an old and crumbling earthenwork dam.

There had been so many rumors over the years about the dam's being unsafe that by now a favorite joke was to yell to a friend in greeting, "Flee to the hills. The dam has burst."

Not that anybody had any notion of what would happen if it *did* burst. Just a few weeks earlier, a leading citizen of Johnstown had been telling friends what to expect if the lake ever became so swollen that the dam gave way. "It might raise the water in the streets here two feet—no more," he had said with great certainty.

The big worry during that last week of May was whether the rain would hold off for the parade.

Early Thursday morning, farmers looked at the sky, gray as pewter, and decided that the promised storm might not break before evening. Usually they only went into town on market day, Saturday, but now they hitched up the horses to buckboard wagons, piled the whole family in, and drove down to see the holiday sights.

Main Street in Johnstown was bright enough to make up for the sullen sky. Store fronts were draped in red, white, and blue bunting. Flags waved from the upper-story windows of lodge rooms: The German–American Society, Ancient Order of Hibernians, Odd Fellows, Masons. Many of the workers in the steel mills were recent immigrants—Hungarians, Poles, Italians, with a few Serbs, Czechs, and Slovaks. They too had their own societies and were flying their own flags along with the Stars and Stripes.

In the park, farmers' wives laid out picnic lunches while their children played around the fountain with its six iron swans hissing and spouting water. In the open stretch beyond, the two boys' baseball teams, the Little Potatoes and the Quicksteps, had worn down the grass practicing, but most of them weren't around that noon. Those who were members of the Boys' Band and the Boys' Drum Corps had already gone home to get into their uniforms.

The cows that grazed in the park as placidly as if it were a pasture had been the subject of some heated arguments that spring. The local paper, the *Tribune*, had reported sternly that bicyclists going through the park at too daring a speed had frightened the cows. Several cyclists had written the editor crossly that cows looming up at night frightened *them*. As a result of this feud, the town council had passed an ordinance forbidding cows or pigs to roam loose after dark in the park.

The council had also discussed, at other meetings, whether to insist that the South Fork Hunting and Fishing Club, which owned the lake and dam, make repairs. But the members of the club were mostly wealthy Pittsburgh men, some of the biggest tycoons in the country, and this was an era when the rich were regarded with nervous awe. So Johnstown's town council kept quiet, and the local governments of the nine smaller boroughs did the

same. Each community had its own burgess (or mayor), its sheriff and other officials. There wasn't any strong central authority to throw the combined weight of ten boroughs behind an important issue, even when it affected them all. But on Memorial Day all the officials were of one mind: They were gathering in Johnstown to join the festivities.

The parade was to start from the Point, where the two rivers came together like the two sides of a triangle, enclosing that end of Johnstown. By

noon, the din there was ear-splitting, as the Boys'
Band, the City Band, and two visiting groups of
tootlers tuned up, with thumping competition from
the Boys' Drum Corps. As the steeple clock on the
Lutheran Church struck two, the first group of
marchers stepped out briskly on schedule, eager to
beat the threatened rain.

The frock-coated burgesses of the boroughs
walked importantly at the head of the parade,
some swinging gold-headed canes. White horses
hauling the fire department's engine wagon flaunted
red ribbons in their harnesses. The Hussar Band
was even more eye-catching in scarlet with flashing
gold braid. Members of the Austrian Society and
other groups of foreign descent wore native folk
costumes of brilliant, embroidered yellows and
greens and reds. Ladies of the Red Cross rode in
open carriages. They had parasols tucked at their
feet ready to be whipped out and used as um-
brellas, if necessary, to protect their best hats. The
hats themselves had brims the size of platters,
heaped with wax fruits and flowers.

If the bands didn't all play in key, at least their
holiday mood was in harmony. A soberer note was
sounded when disabled Civil War veterans rode by,
in the faded blue uniforms of twenty-four years
before. They were followed by a hearse loaded
with muskets, a grim reminder that Memorial Day
honors war's dead.

Even the excited small boys following the parade
out Main Street to the cemetery were respectfully

silent while wreaths were placed and a salute fired over the graves. But children who went with their parents to the final ceremonies that afternoon, in the Opera House, wriggled impatiently by the time the main speaker was halfway through his long oration. Even their parents were restless. Those sitting in the balcony could hear rain already pinging on the roof, and they wanted to get home before the weather grew worse.

The nine hundred members of the audience listened with half an ear as the speaker said solemnly, "Peace has its dangers, as well as war."

Danger was already rising, inch by inch, at the dam.

Warning Signs

The dam had been a jinx from the start, like a great leaky mud whale.

It had been built about fifty years after Johnstown was founded by a Swiss immigrant. In 1793 Joseph Johns had bought a 249-acre tract of land in the Conemaugh Valley, and built a log cabin near the point where the two rivers joined. At that time he hadn't an inkling of the rich veins of ore in the hills rising all around. He pictured a pretty little community with houses perched neatly along the slopes and nestled in the leafy hollow, like the chalets of Switzerland. The hills humped above were thickly green with hemlock, spruce, and pine. There were beautiful groves of poplar, cherry, and ash. White and red oaks spread their great arms over the peaceful countryside.

Johns hired a surveyor to lay out a village and sold lots at ten dollars an acre. Occasionally he traded two lots for a cow. Farmers from all over the valley came to barter their goods and to bring their hides to the tannery. More Swiss immigrants arrived to join the founder. Then came Welsh, Scotch, and Irish settlers. Soon the screech of a sawmill cut through the quiet. Johns applied for a town charter and got it, but the state refused to give him money to build a courthouse with Swiss-style gingerbread trimmings and a cupola topped with a weathervane. Joseph Johns was so outraged by this refusal that he sold all his land in the town named after him, and moved away in the early 1800s.

The English settlers who came next weren't concerned about a fancy courthouse. What they wanted was a forge to smelt the ore in the surrounding hills. That first forge, finished in 1811, was the start of the iron and steel industry.

It started modestly with a few furnaces. For years, Johnstown shipped most of its raw ore down river. Transportation was easy, because the town was a link in the remarkable waterways system of interlocking canals that carried passengers and freight all the way from Pittsburgh to Philadelphia.

The dam was built because the state wanted a reservoir to supply water during dry seasons for the canal from Johnstown to Pittsburgh. In 1840 the Pennsylvania legislature voted seventy thousand dollars for the canal's construction, and surveyors picked a location in the hills twelve miles east of Johnstown. South Fork Run and a dozen other mountain streams would feed the reservoir, and in turn it would feed the canal when rivers were parched in summer.

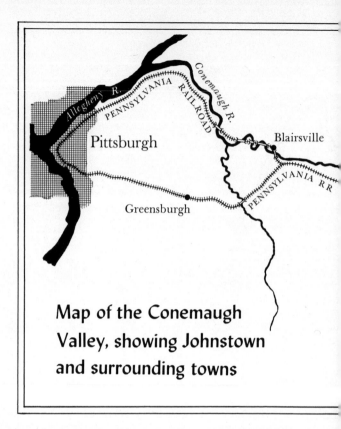

Map of the Conemaugh Valley, showing Johnstown and surrounding towns

The Little Conemaugh runs through Johnstown and becomes the Conemaugh a few miles downstream. And the Conemaugh is a main tributary of the Allegheny, which, like the Monongahela, drains the western watershed of the Allegheny Mountains. The average rainfall is heavier around Johnstown than around Pittsburgh, but often it's a case of flood or drought, and that's the way it was in the 1840s. The rivers, overfed and overflowing in spring, were so shallow in summer that boys could wade across them. But canal boats couldn't wade; they needed a constant level of

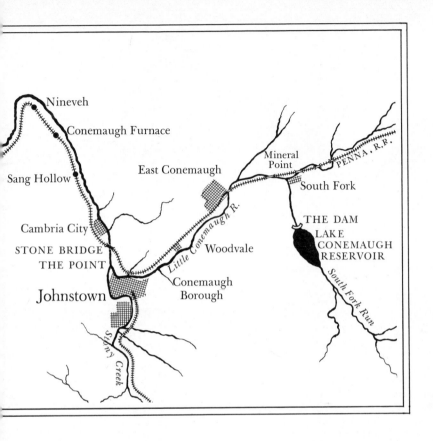

water to navigate in. The new reservoir would supply it.

By the standards of that day, the dam was fairly solid. In fact the contractor said expansively that it would be "as enduring as the Pyramids." The sides, anchored to an old creek bed, rose one hundred feet. The lower part of the wall was stone, reaching up twenty feet above the normal water line. The earth filling was also reinforced by an outer stone wall called riprapping. And a layer of slate put between the stone core and the riprap was supposed to hold the earth filling firmly in place.

Five discharge pipes as big around as barrels, set in the rock culvert at the base, drained off whatever excess water didn't run out the spillway. No water was ever expected to flow over the top.

Unfortunately the sides of the dam kept springing leaks even while it was under construction. After the state had spent far more money and time than anybody had foreseen, the dam was finally finished in 1852. Two years later a steam railway replaced the entire waterways system, and the reservoir quickly became a useless hulk.

In 1857 the state sold its transportation system to the Pennsylvania Railroad for a bargain seven and one-half million dollars, and threw in the dam which nobody wanted. For years it just crumbled away while Johnstown, below, grew into a booming industrial and transportation center. The very thing that had turned the dam into an obsolete nuisance—steam railways—helped the iron and steel industry zoom.

Cambria Iron Works, founded in 1852 and named after the county, made the first 30-foot steel rails and Bessemer steel converter in America.

The Civil War boomed production: armor plate for ships, iron for breach-loading cannons and guns, tracks for a farflung network of railroads to carry supplies and troops. After the war, Cambria manufactured most of the rails that tracked to the west, and even the barbed wire that enclosed the new cattle ranches. The company built more plants, bought out smaller firms, and kept expanding until it rivaled the Carnegie–Schwab–Frick steel combine in Pittsburgh. The Krupps of Germany, the biggest steel makers in the world, began to watch Pennsylvania's two fire-breathing giants with respectful attention.

In peak seasons Cambria employed six thousand men in mills and factories all through the valley. An average week's pay for a 60-hour week was often as low as ten dollars, but Cambria had built hundreds of matchbox houses of raw pine that rented for from five to fifteen dollars a month. Most of these were located along the riverbanks in neighboring boroughs near the plants. Workers who got sick went to the hospital Cambria had built, and were sure of receiving free treatment there if they couldn't pay. The Cambria library even gave the workers free night courses in every subject from mechanical drawing and mathematics to political economy. The mammoth company was so much the Great Provider that when a Sunday School teacher in Johnstown once asked one of her pupils, "Johnny, who made the world?" he answered instantly, "The Cambria Iron Works."

Johnstown had the lowest unemployment rate of any town its size in the country. Officials bragged in speeches about its great share of "prosperity and contentment."

The crumbling old dam had no place in this rosy picture. For more than twenty years, only fishermen and picnickers ever visited the reservoir.

Weeds choked the wagon trail that ran around the
broad top rim. The stone culvert at the base collapsed during heavy rains and washed out sections
of the wall. From then on it was saddle shaped
with a hump in the middle. This meant that water
piled up there and pushed at the weakest spot.

In 1875 a shrewd Pittsburgh promoter, Benjamin
Ruff, bought the 400-acre reservoir and 70 acres of
land around it for two thousand dollars. Ruff knew
exactly what he wanted to do: make a sportsmens'
and vacation retreat for wealthy Pittsburghers. He
called it the South Fork Hunting and Fishing Club.
Only a hundred members were accepted, and they
were glad to pay the stiff initiation fee and dues.
The money was used to build a handsome 47-room
clubhouse, and 16 cottages on the wooded slopes
overlooking the reservoir. The repairs to the dam
itself were so slapdash that no engineer super-
vised the work. Leaks in the sides were stuffed
with tree stumps, rotten leaves, and straw—like a
mammoth bird's nest. The valves that controlled
the five discharge pipes had long since rusted
away, leaving only the spillway to take off water.
And the new owners clamped iron gratings over
the spillway to prevent the bass, pickerel, and trout
in the freshly stocked lake from escaping. The fact
that the gratings prevented most of the water from
running out didn't bother the Pittsburghers. Lake
Conemaugh was, at that time, the biggest artificial
lake in the world—three miles long, a mile wide,
and a hundred feet deep in some spots. Members

sitting on the clubhouse porch in summer looked down at the tranquil blue waters, ideal for fishing, swimming, boating. The club's fifty canoes skimmed along as swiftly as dragonflies. Members raced the sailboats in colorful regattas, while the women watched, and cheered the winners. Two steam yachts huffed and puffed from one end of the lake to the other, often carrying the millionaires who were making industrial history in Pittsburgh: steel tycoons Frick, Mellon, and Carnegie and the merchant Joseph Horne among them. They were people who demanded—and got—privacy. Signs went up all around the dam and through the woods: No Trespassing—For Members Only.

Word percolated uneasily through Johnstown that the repaired dam wasn't strong enough to hold the twenty million tons of water in the newly enlarged lake. But only the head of the Cambria Iron Works, Dan Morrell, dared to tackle the club owners. Morrell was a vigorous, brilliant man who had guided Cambria Iron from shaky infancy to a fifty-million-dollar empire. The Pittsburgh steel kings had so much respect for him that they had elected him president of the American Steel and Iron Association. Morrell was naturally alarmed at the threat of all that water right above the valley where Cambria's enormous holdings were concentrated. He insisted on having Cambria's top engineer, John Fulton, make a thorough inspection of the dam, in the company of three club members and a second engineer brought from Pittsburgh. The report confirmed Morrell's own fears, and he sent it right along to the founder of the club, Ruff. Four paragraphs in the report were of particular importance:

> There appear to me two serious elements of danger in the dam: First, the want of a discharge pipe to reduce or take the water out of the dam for needed repairs. Second, the unsubstantial method of repair, leaving a large leak which appears to be cutting the new embankment.
>
> As the water cannot be lowered, the difficulty arises of reaching the course of the present destructive leaks. At present, there are 40 feet of water in the dam. When the full head of 60 feet is reached it appears to me to be only a question of time until the former cutting is repeated.
>
> Should this break be made during a season of flood, it is evident that considerable damage would ensue along the line of the Conemaugh [River]. It is impossible to estimate how disastrous this flood would be, as its force would depend on the size of the breach in the dam with proportional rapidity of discharge.
>
> The stability of the dam can only be measured by a thorough overhauling of the present lining on the upper slope and the construction of an ample discharge pipe to reduce or remove the water to make necessary repairs.

Ruff read this and wrote back tartly that the

club thought the dam had been sufficiently repaired. His letter ended, "You and your people are in no danger from our enterprise."

Morrell then turned to the Pennsylvania Railroad, because next to Cambria Iron it had the biggest investment around Johnstown. Trains coming from the east followed the course of the Little Conemaugh—from South Fork through Woodvale, East Conemaugh, Conemaugh borough, Johnstown, Cambria City, and on down the river to Pittsburgh. A big marshaling yard and roundhouse were located in East Conemaugh, and the railroad carried three times as much freight from this area as from any other community that size.

The Pennsylvania sent two of its engineers to make an inspection of the dam. One agreed with Cambria's man on the urgent need for repairs. The other said, in effect—Nonsense, everything's dandy. The railroad officials preferred to believe the second report. They didn't want to act as gadflies to millionaires like Frick and Carnegie, who gave so much business to the Pennsylvania line.

Dan Morrell still felt uneasy. He wrote Ruff again, offering to have Cambria Iron pay part of the costs "toward making the dam absolutely safe." The South Fork Hunting and Fishing Club refused to have any work done. After Morrell died in 1885, nobody at Cambria seems to have carried on his long, spunky fight for repairs. This was all too clear when a mine superintendent in the area

went to the county sheriff and told him that the
county should get an injunction against the club,
requiring the owners to reconstruct the dam or
tear it down. The sheriff went instead to consult
Cambria Iron Works officials. With Morrell no
longer alive, they shrugged off the problem.

Their chief engineer, John Fulton, had kept a
copy of his old report, but his superiors must have
considered it too alarmist. Most citizens had been
lulled into the comforting belief that if there were
any real danger, the Cambria Iron Works would
have known and acted to protect its investment.

One skinny, leather-faced woodsman who had a
cabin in the woods beyond the club and served
as caretaker and guide, did his best to warn
the owners. Herb Webber hunted and fished to
earn extra money, and he knew the forest and
streams around South Fork as well as he knew the
back of his hand. He also had a woodsman's eye
for weather signals, and he knew more storms were
on the way. He had seen the dam spouting leaks,
"like a giant watering pot," that last week in
May, 1889, but he didn't dare heckle the president
of the club, Colonel Elias Unger, again. Unger had
told Webber the members were sick and tired of
his nagging. He warned Webber to "shut up about
the dam or be bounced." Unger was president
simply because he was the only member who
lived right near the club. He had been a hotel
manager until he retired and bought property

on South Fork Run. He was flattered to be chosen
president by members so much wealthier than he—
men he considered too important to be worried
with petty details like a leaky dam.

On the Monday before Memorial Day, seventy-
five workmen arrived at the club, armed with picks
and shovels. When Herb Webber saw them, he
thought that at last something was being done to
shore up the dam. Not at all. The workmen were
there to dig sewer trenches for drainage so that
the cottages could have indoor plumbing. Most of
them had been brought in from other communities,
and they stayed in tents pitched on the slopes
above the dam. Colonel Unger kept them digging
right through Memorial Day, because he wanted
to have plumbing in the cottages before warm
weather, when members would begin to come with
their families.

Although he couldn't help worrying about the
condition of the dam, Colonel Unger was eager to
have the fishing as good as ever. If he had the
grating over the spillway removed, to help let the
overflow run out of the dam, the fish would
escape. Before doing anything that might spoil the
fishing, he wanted to consult with the members in
Pittsburgh. Besides, there was a good possibility
that the rain would be over by morning.

On the evening of Memorial Day, while the rain
pelted down, Colonel Unger sat in the big, comfortable clubhouse lounge beside a roaring fire and
wondered if he had been right in taking a chance

that the rain would stop by morning. The club's new resident engineer, John Parke, Jr., encouraged a wait-and-see attitude. Parke was a blond, stocky, pleasant, unimaginative 23-year-old, and this was his first job. In addition to his inexperience, he was so eager to agree with the men who had employed him that he shut his eyes to trouble. "The dam was in perfect condition," he later told a Pittsburgh *Gazette* reporter. In view of the evidence of other witnesses about the leaks, this was an incredible statement. He also said he had been told that it rained very hard that Thursday night but "I slept too soundly myself to hear it."

It did more than rain. Cloudbursts struck all through the mountains. Waterspouts came down like huge shovels and dug up chunks of earth around the lake.

Farmers who had lived around South Fork all their lives said they had never heard anything like it.

John Parke, Jr., didn't hear a thing. But even he knew something was wrong when he went outside after breakfast Friday morning.

I could see there was a flood because the water was over the drive in front of the clubhouse, and the level of water in the lake had risen until it was only 4 feet below the top of the dam. I rode up to the head of the lake and saw that the woods were boiling full of water. South Fork Run and Muddy Run,

which emptied into the lake, were fetching
down trees, logs, cut timber and stuff from
a saw-mill up in the woods.

This was at 7:30 A.M. and the rain was still
coming down.

Colonel Unger, unlike young Parke, hadn't slept
much, and he was too nervous to eat breakfast.
He gulped some coffee, pulled on his rubber boots,
and went out, reluctantly, to have the workmen
lift up the grating over the spillway, at last. He
must have assumed it would be as easy as remov-
ing the stopper from a tub. The men strained and
tugged, but the gratings were so rusty, so weighted
with long-accumulated rocks and branches that
they couldn't be budged.

Unger and Parke conferred worriedly, yelling to
be heard above the roar of the feeder streams
plunging into the lake. They decided to have half
the workmen throw shovels full of earth "in the
face of the dam to strengthen it." At the same
time, Unger sent the rest of the workers to "cut
a sluiceway in the west side." They struck bedrock
at fourteen inches. The shallow new channel carried off only a trickle, and the water in the lake,
Parke reported, "kept rising at the rate of 10
inches an hour." It had no place to go but up.

From 8:00 A.M., the operators in two nearby
railroad telegraph towers kept clicking messages
back and forth about storm damage and the condition of the dam. The Pennsylvania Railroad

had promised to alert Cambria officials if the situation became worse. Operator Dougherty at South Fork tower reported to Pickerill at Mineral Point, the next tower down the line, that the railroad's old watchman had been up at the dam and said "there was great danger." But in Dougherty's own opinion, "there wasn't much danger."

Pickerill was a cautious, well-educated, new breed of telegrapher who observed the rules and went by the book. He trusted the watchman's opinion above Dougherty's. At 10:00 A.M. he sent a messenger to his wife at their house in Mineral Point, asking her to leave at once and take the children up on the mountainside.

Even young engineer John Parke finally knew "it was impossible to save the dam." At 11:30 A.M. he jumped on his horse outside the clubhouse, and ". . . galloped down the road to South Fork to warn the people of their danger." As he raced up and down the streets, yelling, he must have looked and sounded frantic enough to convince the villagers. Most of them piled a few belongings in wagons and got out.

Meanwhile Parke had sent two men to the South Fork telegraph tower, a mile beyond, "to have messages sent to Johnstown and other points below." The overly optimistic operator, Dougherty, was eating his lunch when Parke's two couriers arrived, so they gave the message to his assistant, Miss Emma. Parke said later, "I heard that the lady operator fainted when she sent off the news."

Whether she fainted or not, the message that finally reached Pickerill at Mineral Point only stated that the dam was "in bad condition." Either Miss Emma or Dougherty had watered down the urgent warning that the men were supposed to have brought, or young Parke hadn't worded it strongly enough in the first place.

Pickerill, hearing this message click in over his punch board, was thankful he had already sent his family to safety.

He received another message from South Fork at 1:52 P.M.

> THE WATER IS RUNNING OVER THE BREAST OF LAKE DAM, IN CENTER, AND WEST SIDE IS BECOMING DANGEROUS.
>
> DOUGHERTY

Pickerill knew that when the rollicking Dougherty used the word "dangerous," things were serious.

At 2:25 P.M. the superintendent of a coal mine near South Fork (the same man who had begged the county sheriff earlier to get out an injunction against the club owners) acted on the latest report from an observer he had stationed at the lake.

The message he asked Dougherty to send down the line was:

> THE DAM IS GETTING WORSE AND MAY POSSIBLY GO.
>
> J.P. WILSON

Pickerill received this and instantly put it on the wire for East Conemaugh, asking that the warning be passed along to Conemaugh and Johnstown. He breathed easier when at 2:35 P.M. he got back the call letters of the East Conemaugh operator and knew the message had reached there. Then the line went dead. He waited tensely for more reports from Dougherty at South Fork.

Sometime in the early afternoon Herb Webber, the lanky caretaker, was repairing a cottage porch when he glanced at the lake, saw the level was going down, and wondered if the dam had given way. He ran down the slope and saw it was still holding, but spurting like a fountain from leaks. While he watched, one jet shot out thirty feet, and the water began seeping through the foundation stones. Webber just stood there watching. He made no move to warn the villagers or anybody else. He had been telling people for months that this might happen. He had even told the mayor of Johnstown, who had promised to have a man inspect the dam, and "report to Harrisburg if there was a weakness." Nothing had happened; no inspector had come.

Engineer John Parke had returned from South Fork village to the clubhouse and felt he had done his full duty. As he said later, the men had sent out his message at noon, so "the people of Johnstown should have had three hours warning."

They should have—but most of them didn't.

Friday Morning
in Johnstown

The phone in the Methodist parsonage at Johnstown rang during breakfast on Friday. The Reverend Henry Chapman answered it and came back to tell his wife that old Ross, who belonged to their church, had driven his wagon into a flooded excavation down near the river, and drowned. In all the water-logged history of Johnstown, nobody had ever drowned in a flood before. It seemed like a shocking accident, but not the sort of thing to cause any alarm. The Reverend Mr. Chapman said he wanted to visit the dead man's family that morning, but by the time he started out, the water in front of the parsonage, facing the park, was already three feet deep. A neighbor was sweeping furiously with a broom, trying to keep the dirty water away from the porch.

Boys waded by in rubber boots, splashing happily and grabbing at logs to ride bareback. Rains had washed out a log boom during the night. Hundreds of logs swirled in the muddy brown river, and floated over the banks into town. Youngsters and grown men were roping them together to make rafts. Already the lower end of Johnstown looked like a crazy kind of Venice, with citizens hailing each other from the tipsy rafts, or going up and down the sidewalks in rowboats.

One rower paddled over to chat with Mr. Chapman. The man offered to come back in his boat during the afternoon and take the minister over to call on Ross's widow, if the streets were still flooded.

Mr. Chapman went back to his study and chose the text for his sermon for Sunday: "Man dieth and wasteth away; yea, man giveth up the ghost and where is he?" He was scratching away with a quill pen when his wife's cousin, Mrs. Brinker, who lived across the park, burst in crying, "The water's already coming up our street and the reservoir will break and we'll all be swept away."

As Mr. Chapman wrote later, "I was so incredulous I could have laughed if she hadn't been so much frightened."

He told her soothingly, "You've been hearing this for years and it hasn't happened yet. I don't think there's much danger. But if you fear that your house will be flooded, ours stands higher and I believe will be safe."

Mrs. Brinker, somewhat calmed, agreed to spend the day there. She and the Chapmans' 7-year-old granddaughter, Nellie, who was there on a month's visit, sat at the window watching the sights. The Reverend Mr. Chapman had barely settled down to work on his sermon again when his wife came in to report that their German maid was behaving rather peculiarly. The girl spoke almost no English, but she had evidently caught Mrs. Brinker's hysteria. Now she was running up to the attic every five minutes to store provisions there. She had already carted up bread, cold meat, matches, and jugs of water and milk.

Exasperated by all this female foolishness, Mr. Chapman said, "Well, she'll just have to carry it all down again tonight."

By then Mrs. Brinker was fretting because her husband had insisted on staying at home. The Brinkers had no phone so she couldn't call to ask if the water in the cellar had reached her preserve shelf.

The phone was such a newfangled invention that there were only three hundred in the entire valley community. Most of them were in offices, stores, and plants. Doctors and ministers, and a few wealthy families, had the others. Calls buzzed to a record peak that Friday, and the phone in the Cambria company's general office kept jangling as managers of the various mills called in to report. The lower plant, in Cambria City, the borough just below Johnstown, had closed down at 7:00 A.M. Water was already a foot deep, lapping at the machinery. The other mills sent their workers home by midmorning. Only maintenance crews stayed on duty to keep the steam up and the furnaces fired.

Frederick Krebs, a manager of the Gautier Wire

Works, which had been taken over by Cambria, told the men jokingly that they would probably work harder at home than at the plant, because their wives would have chores lined up. In flood time, taking up carpets and moving prized knickknacks to safety were as automatic as spring housecleaning.

Krebs had to walk home. The horse-drawn streetcars had stopped running early when water washed over the tracks. By the time he had hiked back from the plant in Conemaugh, the borough which bordered Johnstown on the west, his wife had dinner ready. In Johnstown, as in most of the country, people who could eat at home had a hearty midday dinner, with supper in the evening. That noon the Krebs' table was piled even more lavishly than usual in honor of a visiting relative from West Virginia: four kinds of vegetables; beef, chicken, and ham; a choice of hot breads; pickalilli relish, elderberry jelly, wild plum jam. The host heaped food onto plates and said genially, "Let's enjoy this meal. It may be a long time before we get another like it." The two women laughed at what they considered just another family joke.

Cambria's general counsel, Cyrus Elder, was a debonair man famous for his sense of humor, but at the moment he was sitting gloomily in the company's main office, worrying about his wife and daughter. He had returned during the morn-

ing from a business trip to New York, and found
that his house, in the lower end of town, was
already surrounded by water. The women were
alone there, and it made him uneasy. He felt even
more uneasy as Cambria's vice-president, Powell
Stackhouse, brought him up to date on the trouble
at South Fork reservoir. Stackhouse said that for
three days the dam had been leaking badly. If
the break came, the Pennsylvania Railroad tower
at South Fork would flash a warning right down
the line—from Mineral Point to East Conemaugh
to Woodvale to Conemaugh to Johnstown. Cambria's executive offices were connected by phone to
all the railroad's telegraph towers and to the local
Western Union. This made the alarm system
doubly certain. The instant any warning came, the
maintenance crews left at the plants were to tie
down all whistles to sound an alarm for the
townspeople, so they could move up to high
ground. Both Cyrus Elder and Stackhouse took it
for granted that the Cambria factories themselves
weren't in real danger. A few extra feet of flood
water—and they still thought that that was the
most a broken dam could cause—sounded puny
when compared with the company's vast domain.
The blast furnaces in the borough of Millville,
for instance, had 75-foot stacks and 40 boilers to
generate steam. In a nearby open hearth building,
a 10-ton traveling crane moved like a fabulous
iron monster. The brick factory of the Gautier
Wire Works in Conemaugh sat as solidly as

Gibraltar. The lower plant, in Cambria City below Johnstown, was just as massive. Cambria was a kingdom that could never be toppled by water.

Although Cyrus Elder was sure of that, he still felt nervous about his family. At two o'clock, he started for home in a skiff, with two employees paddling. The Reverend Mr. Chapman, passing by in a rowboat on his way to visit the Ross family, saw the skiff tilt and turn over, as a strong current rushed from a side street. Cyrus Elder stood up, hip-deep in water, and called cheerfully, "Have you got any fishing tackle, Reverend? I might as well make use of my time here."

A high-wheeled wagon came along, and the driver gave Elder a lift. When he tried to make the horse turn down Walnut Street, to Elder's house, the animal reared up, neighing in terror as water reached his haunches. Elder had to stop at his brother's, where he borrowed some dry clothes and comforted himself remembering how solid his own brick house was.

Another prominent lawyer of Johnstown, Horace Rose, hitched up his buggy right after breakfast and took his two youngest sons downtown to buy them raincoats. Then the boys came to his office and helped him move papers in bottom drawers to higher places. The flood of 1887, two years earlier, had left twelve inches of water and soaked some legal briefs.

Nobody wanted a lawyer that day; the law couldn't order rivers to stop running over. On the way home, Rose yelled *Whoa!* and stared at the odd sight in the middle of the street. A cow being led to higher ground had stopped and was drinking placidly, as if at a farm trough. He called to a passer-by, "Charley, you and I have lived here fifty years and this is the first time we ever saw a cow drink Stony Creek water on Main Street."

It was also the first time the two rivers, Stony Creek and the Little Conemaugh, had overflowed at once. That was partly because the channels had been getting narrower every year, as Cambria plants dumped ashes and refuse along the banks. The town council had always permitted this filling in, but Rose now decided that it was time to put a stop to the practice. As one of the few Democrats in town, he wasn't as awed by the Republican steel and iron tycoons as most people. A big man with a jutting nose and jaw, as well as a former district attorney of the county, he was bursting with civic indignation. When he met a neighbor who was also the town treasurer, Rose suggested in his booming voice that they form a citizens' committee to insist the channels be widened again, especially below the point where the two rivers joined.

At dinner Rose explained this plan to his admiring family. Of his five children, only Forrest, the 16-year-old, was absent, visiting a friend across the street. Even the Roses' married son, Horace, Jr., had come over to help move furniture. Rose was rather cross because the expensive new dining-room wallpaper showed stains along the baseboard. By then the floor was so damp, as water seeped up from the cellar, that the family moved to an upstairs sitting room. The boys built a fire in the grate; their mother made coffee and served it in the tin cups they used for picnics. Soon even Rose was in a picnic mood. He tied a bag of candy to the end of a broom and leaned out the window to pass it to a little girl in the next house. All along the street, people were hanging out of bedroom windows, joking and chatting with neighbors. Percy, the youngest Rose boy, pointed excitedly to rats running across the tops of fences, but nobody considered this an ominous sign. In fact his father got a rifle and amused himself by shooting at the fleeing rats. The water was already going down, and he told Percy they would check the level again at 4:15. Not once did he think of the dam.

At the *Tribune* office downtown, where both the daily and weekly newspapers were printed, the white-haired editor, George Swank, was rereading a memo from his city editor. It said, "The Central Telephone Office called to say it had been informed by Agent Deckert of the Pennsylvania Railroad freight station that the South Fork reservoir was getting worse all the time and that the danger of its breaking was increasing momentarily."

Swank reached for a pad and started an editorial, "It is idle to speculate what would be the result if this tremendous body of water . . . should be thrown into the already submerged valley of the Conemaugh."

In the city room, Assistant Editor George Gibbs was writing a running account of the flood, to appear whenever the *Tribune* could come out again. He thought that would probably be the next day, after the city had dried out. The office was on the second floor over the post office, in the heart of town, so that Gibbs had had a first-hand view.

> As we write at noon, Johnstown is again under water and all about us the tide is rising. Wagons have for hours been passing along the streets, carrying people from submerged points to places of safety, and boats, floating as jauntily as upon ᐧ the bosom of a river, have traversed the thoroughfares in the lower part of town, removing pent-up inmates from homes. We hear of . . . the Rolling Mill shut down, costly bridges swept away, great landslides which lock the railroads, penning in trains where they were forced to stop upon the track . . . cellars filled the whole town over, the streets as far up and back as Jackson running over with the yellow, devastating flood. A most exasperating state of affairs, and one for which there ought to be a remedy. . . .

Almost every business in town had closed down, but the newspaper office hummed, as did the main offices of Central Telephone and Western Union.

They shared the ground floor of a building on Washington Street backing on the river. Operators at Central Telephone had already called all three hundred subscribers to warn them that the dam was weakening. One of the few citizens who took this seriously, and acted on it, was Dix Tittle. His wife had died a few months earlier, so he felt all the more responsible for their children. When the rumors began buzzing along the wire, he insisted that the two boys and their two sisters go up on one of the hills that rose all around Johnstown like the sides of a bowl. Dix, Jr., remembered later how cheated he felt, a 12-year-old marooned under a tree on the hill in the rain, while down below in Johnstown his friends were having a day of water sport in the streets. There were several dozen other people clumped under trees like the Tittles, and they all acted rather embarrassed. Dix, for one, dreaded facing his friends afterward and having them yell "Fraidy cat." As one survivor said sadly later, "It got so that people were more afraid of being called coward then they were of the dam."

A Pittsburgh lumber merchant, in town that day on business, thought the local people were taking the warnings much too casually. He stood with a group reading a bulletin pasted on the board outside the Western Union office. It said that, because of rains and high water, the dam was so weakened it might give way. The others seemed unimpressed, but the out-of-towner felt so nervous that he decided to catch the next train home.

Inside the Western Union office, nobody was panicky. The manager, Hetty Ogle, had ordered her staff to stay on duty "because we may be needed." The three young messengers and the operators she herself had trained wouldn't have dreamed of disobeying little Mrs. Ogle. They adored her.

She was a widow in her forties, as cheerfully plump and matter-of-fact as a robin. Her husband had been killed in the Civil War, leaving her with

three children and almost no money. She had gone
to work for Western Union and done so well she
had been made manager of the Johnstown office,
the only woman to hold that job. Along with her
bustling, rather bossy manner, she was enormously
warm-hearted. She had given free training in
telegraphy to fifty local boys and girls and found
jobs for most of them in Western Union's various
branches. The company was so fond of her they
had just paid for repainting her house. It always
overflowed with friends and apprentices and people
wanting Hetty Ogle's advice. A few years before,
when she had had a serious operation, Cambria
ordered the whistles in every plant muted to show
the company's concern. The hospital had to issue
two bulletins a day on her progress for the anxious
townspeople. When she first came out of the operating room, she was too ill to talk. But her son,
sitting beside her bed, saw her fingers tap out
Morse code on the blanket. "I am safe," she was
signaling. "Tell . . . " And she named a relative
she knew would worry.

Her daughter Minnie worked as an assistant in
the office. She was a delicately lovely girl with big
dark eyes and short silky curls like a faun's.
About two o'clock she and the operators and messengers saw the river water seeping in. Mrs. Ogle's
sister, the town librarian, who worked in the
building next door, came in again to ask if they
should all leave, but Hetty still stood firm. Her
son, the assistant postmaster, had already phoned

three times, begging her to get away from the riverbank. Mrs. Ogle reported to the Pittsburgh operator that things were getting too wet on the ground floor and that she and her staff would move to the third floor until the river went down. While the wire was still open, she sent a last message to the manager of the Pittsburgh office:

SOUTH FORK OPERATOR SAYS THE DAM IS ABOUT TO GO

About the same time, two young men, Alexander Adair and Richard Eyre, stood in dismay at the place where the bridge should have been, connecting Cambria City to Johnstown. They had crossed it a few hours before to inspect some property they owned. The men weren't too alarmed, because every year a few wooden bridges floated off in flood time. But it meant they would have to walk all the way home on the railroad tracks. A westbound freight tooted, and as Adair and Eyre leaped aside, the engineer shouted, "They've just got a warning in East Conemaugh that the dam might break any minute. Pass the word along and run to the hill."

His two listeners were more impressed by his frantic voice than they were by the familiar threat. They decided, reluctantly, to return to Cambria City and deliver the engineer's message. But most of the people they approached on the streets only shrugged and said, "We've heard that one before."

Still doggedly trying, Adair and Eyre went to the mayor's office. Burgess O'Neill wasn't much interested. He agreed politely to spread the word, but he said people wouldn't pay any attention to such an old story.

By that time, Adair and Eyre were tired of trying to be Paul Reveres—especially since nobody listened to them. Going back along the tracks, they crossed at Stone Bridge, a great new seven-span structure built by the Pennsylvania Railroad, just below the Point where the two rivers joined. The men stood there for a few minutes to check the water level: It was falling. They agreed that the dam would probably hold, as it always had, because the flood was ebbing. The idea of going home to a warm bath and a hot toddy appealed to them much more than squatting on some rainy hill. Then they passed a man from Millville who changed their minds again. He had heard the same warning that Adair and Eyre had received from the engineer, and he said it was no false alarm. Adair and Eyre left the tracks and headed up the nearest hill. It was then 3:15.

Six-year-old Gertrude Quinn and her sisters listened round-eyed during dinner when their father told them not to stir from the house, and to be ready to "go to the hill" if he gave the signal. The Quinns' comfortable, big 3-story house was at the opposite end of town from the Stone Bridge. Green Hill was so close, only a few hun-

dred yards away, that the five young Quinns had
played there all their lives.

Gertrude, the most tomboyish of the girls, had
climbed trees in the woods and had chased her
dog Trump hunting rabbits. Her parents had often
scolded her for her climbing activities, but nobody
could be cross for long at the lively, flyaway child.
She had hair as blond and silky as thistledown.
(Her father called her, "My little whitehead.")
And her dark blue eyes recorded what she saw
like a camera. Almost fifty years afterward, she
wrote one of the most vivid accounts of the flood,
as a record for her grandchildren.

Her memories reached back affectionately to the
days before the flood when life had seemed so
unshakably safe. Her father, uncle, and grandfather
owned the biggest dry goods store in Johnstown.
In an era when every small girl kept a button
collection, and added new ones like jewels, Gertrude and her sisters were the envy of their
schoolmates. The clerks in their father's store kept
them supplied with these treasures. Another uncle
owned a confectionery store and handed out
an endless stream of free candy. And a child like
Gertrude could supply her own delicious mischief.
She remembered the Election Night when she had
climbed up on the roof of the house with her
adored 16-year-old brother Vincent to watch the
torchlight parade. Vincent had held her up,
shaking her and yelling, "Give three cheers for
President Benjamin Harrison." The small girl in

the long flannel nightgown cheered lustily.

It was Vincent who advised her jokingly to temper her frequent spankings by slipping a pie pan under her panties. Gertrude thought this was splendid advice. Her father, when he whacked her behind with a rolled-up newspaper, heard "a drumming on tin" and had a hard time keeping from laughing.

On the Friday of the flood, James Quinn wasn't laughing at all. He was one of the few men who had been worrying constantly about the dam. A few days earlier, he and his wife had gone to a niece's christening in a nearby town, and then he had hurried right back while his wife stayed on. He was too nervous about the dam to feel like a holiday. Customers complained that Mr. Quinn was talking too gloomily.

His sister-in-law, who was visiting the Quinns, said the same thing. She and her 2-year-old son, along with the baby's nurse, had arrived from Kansas the week before. Aunt Abbie, as Gertrude called her, was twenty-four and very pretty. And she brandished opinions as sharp as hat pins. She told her brother-in-law tartly that he was talking nonsense, predicting that the dam might put them in danger. Since she was from flat, dry Kansas, the notion was simply too fantastic for her to accept. She remarked to the nurse, "Mr. Quinn is too fearful. This big brick house would never go."

James Quinn's pointed beard quivered with

annoyance. If the reservoir did burst, he said, "not a brick would stand in the town." The only reason he hadn't already moved his children was that his youngest child, Marie, shouldn't be out in the rain. She was in bed in a darkened room with measles. Before he went back to the store to transfer some merchandise to upper floors, he reminded the children again not to go off the porch. Gertrude sat on the top step, and thought of her brother Vincent downtown wading. She longed to be with him. Yearningly she eyed the flooded yard covered with "yellow gurgling water." The nurse had already yanked her out of the water once that day and had changed her sopping-wet clothes.

The air that afternoon was heavy with "a mist

like the smoke of brushwood fires." She watched the drowned pansies in the flower bed, "little purple faces floating." Vincent's ducks, which he kept behind the barn, came swimming around to the front lawn, quacking joyfully. It was too much for a spirited child to resist. She slid off the steps again and paddled after the swimmers.

"Gertrude!" her father thundered. He had returned just in time to see his daughter imitating a duck.

He told her to go upstairs and get into dry shoes and stockings, and to hurry, because he'd decided they must go up to the hill at once. Even little measle-dotted Marie would have to go with them. "I went through the door in double-quick time, while well-directed blows from his open hand were landing on me."

While she was upstairs, her father waited on the porch, smoking a cigar. He said later that some instinct made him keep looking in the direction of the dam.

The Dam Bursts

Just after three o'clock, the water pounding at the weakened front wall of the dam cut a slice ten feet deep out of the center. A small crowd of workmen, the young engineer, John Parke, and the club's president, Colonel Unger, stood on the slope above watching helplessly as the wild force of twenty million tons of water rushed toward that break. At 3:10, the wall of the dam burst open with a thundering roar. One watcher said, "When Colonel Unger saw the dam go, realizing the awful consequences of the break, he became so ill he had to be assisted back to the club."

The whole lake began to move, then rushed through the opening with a force that made the hills quake. It carried along a 300-foot section of dam wall, to batter against everything in its path.

Two families who lived right below South Fork reservoir had been warned hours before of the danger. One, George Fisher, had moved his wagon, cow, and plow to higher ground. But he and his family barely got out before the mountain of water tore down upon them.

The second farmer, George Lamb, waited until he heard the roaring water and saw neighbors racing down the hill. He yelled to them to get his wife and children while he ran to save his two pigs. He was nearly swept off with the pigsty. The rescuers who had pulled his family to high ground caught Lamb just as the crashing wave descended. He saw his house "climb the face of the great wall of water . . . roll and toss for an instant with Fisher's house, and then they were flung against the bluff with a force that dashed them to splinters."

After smashing against the steep hill, the wave bounded back and washed over the evacuated village of South Fork. Engineer John Parke's frantic warning at noon had sent some of the villagers scrambling for safety. Others had moved out when the swollen river washed over the streets. A mile away, railroad telegraph operator Dougherty, who had been so skeptical that morning, leaped out and ran for the hill. He made his escape just seconds before the massive wave toppled his tower.

Just west of South Fork Village, the Chicago–New York Limited had been flagged to a halt many hours earlier because of the landslide farther down the line. Workmen had been working all day to clear the tracks, and the fuming engineer kept watch, waiting for the signal to proceed. When he saw the flood water charging down on the village, he started up the train with almost

miraculous speed. It hurtled across the river just
before the flood wave hit the bridge, swallowing
it whole, along with the freight cars at the end
of the train.

So far, the flood had snatched only a few
victims, sweeping them downstream while they
clung to a roof or a barn floor. A trainman cut
off a bell cord to use as a tow line, and he and
some passengers ran to the riverbank to help. "We
saved some and we could have saved more, but
they were afraid to let go of the debris."

The wave went bounding on down the valley,
rolling giant boulders like pebbles, snapping off
75-foot-high trees, yanking up groves of maples and
birches edging the banks.

Five miles below the dam, the village of Mineral
Point nestled between two hills, with neat little
white clapboard houses clustered around the wood-
working plant of the Cambria Iron Works. Only
a watchman was on duty at the plant, and he
was one of sixteen victims. There would undoubtedly
have been more, but the flood wave was now so
clogged with trees and rocks that it ground almost
to a halt at the narrow entrance between the
hills. In those precious moments, a hundred people
raced for safety before the great mass gathered
fresh force and charged. A survivor said, "The
water didn't come down like a wave. It *jumped*
on the houses and beat them to fragments."

Those who couldn't escape in time included an
old lady in a wheel chair and the daughter who

had refused to desert her, a mother and six
children, and a man who had delayed, fatally, in
order to run to his stable and lead out his horses.

The family of William Pickerill, the railroad
telegraph operator at Mineral Point, had been the
first to leave that morning when the urgent message
came: *Get to the hill.*

But Pickerill himself, in the tower to the west
of the village, wouldn't desert his post. There had
been no more messages from Dougherty at South
Fork. The line seemed to be dead. He sat at his
telegraph keyboard, wondering and worrying over
the silence. Through the back window, he could
see a locomotive halted on the tracks just behind
the train. The engineer was waiting for instructions
on whether to proceed to South Fork. Suddenly
Pickerill heard the roar of the flood torrent. Then
a half-dozen bodies came down the river below
the tower, "bobbing like corks."

He tried frantically to reach the East Conemaugh
operator, but no answering signal came through.
Before Pickerill jumped from the swaying telegraph
tower, he shouted to the locomotive engineer,
"The dam broke—clear out or you'll be washed
away." Engineer Hess pulled the steam throttle
wide open, tied down his whistle, and raced his
engine backward all the way into East Conemaugh.
Hundreds of people heard the screeching locomotive
whistle—the first unmistakable warning of danger
—and began to run for the hill that slanted up
150 yards behind the railroad station. With the

whistle still shrieking, Hess braked to a halt near the marshaling yard, leaped out, and ran up Railroad Street to snatch his family. By the time he had hustled them up the slope, the flood was tossing his engine around like a toy.

The entire roundhouse and twenty-nine locomotives, plus boxcars and storage sheds piled with equipment, were carried off in the grinding, whirling water.

A hundred passengers on the Day Express, which had left Pittsburgh early that morning, had been sitting since 10:00 A.M. in East Conemaugh, held up by the same landslide that had halted the eastbound Limited. There were two sections, sitting on separate tracks. The first section consisted of five day coaches, a Pullman, a baggage car, and a mail train at the rear. In the second section the gayest, most unconcerned passengers of all were two pretty, lively 20-year-old girls who had come from a wedding. They still wore the corsages pinned on their jackets. Bessie Bryan had been visiting Jennie Paulson in Pittsburgh during the wedding festivities. Now Jennie was going to Bessie's home in Philadelphia, where a house party was already arranged. A passenger who sat behind them could hear the two chatting merrily about what so-and-so wore at the wedding, and which young men were expected at the house party. When they ran out of chatter, which seldom, Jennie would open a novel and read a chapter while Bessie looked out the window at the river, which was as yellow as boiling taffy.

About 3:30 P.M., the shriek of a train whistle, wailing nonstop, made even Jennie, deep in her novel, glance up. The conductor came into the coach and said in a quiet voice, "Please step up on the hillside as quickly as possible." He snatched up two young children and went trotting out the other end of the car. Jennie and Bessie followed, but when they reached the platform, Jennie looked down at the oozing mud below, then pointed to her light kid slippers and made a face. As the conductor shouted, "Don't wait for anything," both girls turned back for their overshoes and raincoats. That precious minute cost them their lives.

A man from New Jersey, William Schreder, who was in the Pullman behind the coaches, said that when he ran out on the platform he was horrified at the sight.

> It seemed as though a forest was coming down on us. A great wall of water was roaring and grinding, so thickly studded with trees it resembled a gigantic avalanche. . . . That instant, I saw an engine lifted bodily off the tracks and thrown backward into the whirlpool, houses crushed in the flash of an eye, and the noise like constant thunder. I shouted to the ladies in the car, three of them alone, to fly for their lives and helped them out. Two others jumped the ditch, through which

water was running swiftly, but the third, a heavy lady, a missionary on her way to a foreign post, hesitated. While I was holding out my hand and urging her to jump, the water swept her into the torrent. . . . The water was about my knees as I clambered up the hill. Ten seconds later when I looked back, it was surging and boiling ten feet deep over the track I'd just left. . . .

An old man, a cripple, started slowly down the steps of a coach. When he realized he was blocking the way of a woman behind him, he threw himself down the steps to give her a chance to escape. A conductor snatched him up and carried him on his back until a wave tore the old man loose.

At least two conductors took to their heels as soon as they heard Engineer Hess's whistle, and reached the hill ahead of everybody else, "with their white caps unmuddied." When newspapers later carried stories saying that the conductors had gone through every car telling passengers to flee, there was a bitter outcry from survivors who had had no warning at all. But at least part of the crew behaved coolly and bravely. A Negro chef and two porters were heroic, staying in the cars until the last possible second to see that women and children escaped.

A passenger in the second section, standing on the back of the platform, heard the warning and rushed back to the seat where his wife and baby were sitting. He told a reporter later:

Grasping the child, I called to my wife to follow me. The water was like a huge wall, not five hundred feet from us. Everybody jumped. It was every man for himself and God for us all. I ran with my child in my arms and my wife close behind. I came to a small creek that had become swollen and jumped over that, then I looked for my wife. When she got to the creek she hesitated at first, but a man behind her called out, "Jump, jump, for Heavens sake!" That determined her, and she jumped and cleared the creek. The water was close behind us but we succeeded in getting away.

All their baggage was lost, of course, but that didn't bother the fleeing passenger. "Thank God," he said, "I have my wife and child. The way in which the water hurled that train to destruction was terrible."

A flooded gully between the train and the hill was an even worse death trap. Some passengers managed to cross on the rickety wooden planks, but many fell in and were drowned. A doctor from Port Royal, Pennsylvania, described how he got across and then heard screams.

[Nine women were] struggling in the ditch with water up to their armpits. I instantly grabbed the hand of the first and quickly pulled her out. All the others reached for me at once. I succeeded in saving them all except for one old lady. I said to her, "Give me your

hand—quick." She evidently was bewildered,
for she replied, "I will go this way," and
walking toward the maddened waters, she was
lost.

Another passenger, Dr. Robinson, a professor
from the Theological Seminary in Allegheny,
Pennsylvania, had sat calmly in the train making
neat notes of the day's events in a journal, to
show to his wife when he returned. His car was
one of those which received no warning except for
Engineer Hess's whistle. The professor managed to
get to the foot of the hill; several people who had
fallen were crawling up the last stretch on their
hands and knees. Robinson later reported on what
he had seen when he looked back:

> What an awful sight presented itself; houses
> falling and sweeping downstream; some six or
> eight rods away two men were dragging a
> woman with all their might; one car broken
> loose and going downstream in plunging
> water, two men on top, others inside. It was
> awful to see the men as the car rolled from
> side to side, trying to keep on top. Then all
> the trains started down the river. I cried out
> in anguish. "They are gone!" They went
> about 500 feet, and were stopped very
> strangely, our engine being lifted up and flung
> upon the head of the other train. Engines
> from the roundhouse were rolled down against
> it, a mass of trees was lodged there, and a
> breakwater formed. . . .

Two cars and the mail train were carried on down. Thirty-seven passengers and crewmen were lost from the Day Express.

A pair of newlyweds on their honeymoon had one of the most harrowing adventures of all the train's survivors. Young Charles Richwood and his bride of one day, Edith, had expected to be in New York that night, and during the dreary long hours of sitting in the stalled train, they had thought longingly of the bridal suite waiting for them in a Fifth Avenue hotel. When they heard Hess's engine whistle screeching, Richwood went to the back platform of his car and saw "a seething, turbulent wall of water, whose crests seemed mountain high, filling the entire valley and carrying everything before it . . ."

As he ran back to get his wife, the wave sucked their Pullman car in. Richwood wrote later:

> With one hand I grasped my wife around the waist, and with the other held onto the window-casing like grim death, vainly trying to resist the terrible rush of water which instantly filled the car. [He managed to get the window open, and pushed his wife through, then followed her.] We at once found ourselves making the most dizzy and fantastic convolutions in our struggle up to the surface. Up and up and up we went. We were drawn upon the floating body of a car, perhaps our own sleeper, now containing three persons, two men and one woman.

Edith Richwood was stunned and nearly unconscious. Her husband was trying frantically to revive her and at the same time hold both of them on the swaying, spinning, plunging Pullman. Debris kept slamming against them, nearly knocking them off the top of the car: dead pigs and cows, mammoth tree trunks, a section of the iron bridge, boxcars, floating roofs. Finally Edith opened her eyes and clung to him. Just then, the "car crashed against some obstruction and we were thrown off. But here again Providence intervened and we were soon assisted on a large float containing about twenty persons. Some there were with crushed and mangled limbs, others were bruised, torn, and almost naked."

The flood was following the river but smashing over the banks to reach houses set farther in.

The Richwoods were being whirled along in the main torrent toward the huge Gautier Wire Works in Conemaugh borough. Richwood saw the boilers spouting "an awful hissing of steam." Tons of hot metal poured into the water, like molten lava from a volcano. He saw workmen scalded horribly. They struggled in the water, then went under. Bale after bale of the barbed wire manufactured in the plant was unwinding in the current, slashing at flesh and clothing, and trussing up victims, while the steam spurted death.

Richwood decided they would prefer being drowned to being scalded to death, and he grabbed a plank floating by. The young couple swung onto it and pushed away from the impromptu raft, which continued straight down toward the cauldron of the Gautier Wire Works.

> Clinging to each other, with our light float between us, we now heard ourselves being encouraged by those on the bank who had witnessed our desperate struggle. As we passed a point some fifty feet from shore we saw one of these sturdy fellows, stripped to the waist, plunge into the water and with long, swift strokes succeed in reaching us.

By then the Richwoods were too exhausted to help themselves, but their deliverer pulled them to shore, "where willing hands tenderly cared for us."

They had been carried down through the wildest devastation the flood had wrought so far. Woodvale, just below East Conemaugh, was the prettiest of all the towns skirting Johnstown proper. On Maple Avenue a leafy long archway of trees shaded the handsome houses.

At about 3:40 P.M., the mayor of Woodvale, Burgess Evans, and a dozen other men, stood on the bridge which connected their town with East Conemaugh. They were talking about the earlier rumors, and debating whether the dam would really go, when a roaring sound gave the answer. The men all scattered to rescue their families. Mayor Evans sprinted three blocks to his house. As he rushed in the door, his oldest boy, a 10-year-old, called from upstairs, "Oh, Papa! The bridge is coming down with lots of stuff."

Evans grabbed three of the younger children; his wife carried two little ones, and the 10-year-old and 8-year-old trotted behind. They ran out the back door, heading toward the hill across the railroad track. In the rush, Evans dropped one of the three small children. A woman just behind them scooped up the baby, and they kept on running. Of all the men who had been on the bridge ten minutes before, Evans was the only one whose whole family was saved. The flood wave smashed down the length of Maple Avenue and laid it "bare as a granite block." The whole town was flattened like a cardboard village. Only one wall of Cambria's big woolen mill was left standing. This was the mill that employed mostly the wives, daughters, and widows of Cambria workmen. They had all been sent home at noon by the foreman. He and the watchman, trapped in the teetering mill, threw out ropes like lassos and caught two women floating past on driftwood. Then all four clung to the remaining wall and were saved.

Robert Miller of Woodvale told a New York *Times* reporter a few days afterward about his experience. He and a friend had gone to the bridge at the other end of town to see if it seemed secure in high water.

> I looked up and saw a dark object up the river. Over it was a mist. It was high and somehow dreadful. Dark smoke seemed to form a background. We didn't wait for more. By instinct we knew the big dam had burst and its water was coming upon us.

His companion jumped on a horse and tried to ride toward Johnstown, yelling warnings as he went. But the flood overtook him and he had to abandon his horse and climb a high hill.

> I went straight to my house in Woodvale, warning everybody as I ran. My wife and mother-in-law were ready to move, with my five children, so we went for the hillside, but

we were not speedy enough. The water had
come over the flat at its base and cut us off.
My wife and I climbed in a coal car with
one of the children to get out of the water.
I put two more children into the car and
looked around for my other children and
mother-in-law. My mother-in-law was a stout
woman, weighing about two hundred and
twelve pounds. She could not climb into a
car. The train was too long for her to go
around it, so she tried to crawl under leading
the [remaining two] children.

The train was suddenly pushed forward by
the flood . . . I never saw my two children
and mother-in-law after the flood first struck
the train of coal cars.

On one of the side streets in Woodvale, a housewife was setting out coffee and bread on the
kitchen table, for a tramp who had knocked at the
back door. She heard people shouting something
about "dam." The tramp quickly herded the two
children out the door and uphill, while their
mother insisted on staying behind long enough to
lock the door. She barely escaped in time; the
key was the only thing left of the house.

Thirty horses shut in the streetcar company's
barn neighed pitifully as they were carried to their
death.

Of the eleven hundred people who lived in
Woodvale, nearly three hundred perished.

The flood wave was now forty feet high, and it

was cutting a valley of death along the river. The torrent hit the town of Conemaugh after Woodvale. In ten minutes the entire lower half of the town was wiped out. Johnstown was next.

The Flood
Hits Johnstown

At ten minutes after four, the flood wave came crashing down the river channel into Johnstown. Then it split into two deadly prongs. One pounded ahead the length of the town, to the Point and the Stone Bridge. The other went smashing sideways to Stony Creek. "The whole city was one surging and whirling mass of water," a survivor said. "It swept away house after house with a rapidity the eye could not follow."

Tow-headed little Gertrude Quinn was still upstairs changing into dry clothes. Her father stood on the porch, smoking his cigar in impatient puffs while waiting to escort his small daughters to Green Hill. As Gertrude wrote later, "He looked out and saw a blur . . . like dust that precedes a cavalry charge and heard at the same time an ominous sound that froze the marrow of his bones."

He ran indoors shouting, "Follow me straight to the hill. Run for your lives."

He snatched up measle-spotted Marie, wrapped her in a blanket, and carried her downstairs, followed by his daughters Helen and Rosemary. His sister-in-law Abbie was to carry her little boy, and their nurse would bring Gertrude. When Abbie protested, James Quinn told her, "We cannot take the chance of staying here."

As he went down the street with Rosemary at his side, the little girl was splashing through water almost up to her neck, and holding an umbrella over her head. The photographic mind of 6-year-old Gertrude recorded this odd sight while she was yanking at the nurse, wanting to follow. But as they started down the steps, her aunt said petulantly, "I do not like to put my feet into that dirty water. We may catch cold and get sick and die." She told the nurse that they would go to the playroom on the third floor instead, and repeated, "This big house will never move."

The nurse carried Gertrude, who squirmed frantically, screaming and kicking, trying to get free and run after her father. When she was let down in the playroom, she rushed to the front window. Her father and sisters were already out of sight, but what she saw and heard was etched on her mind forever:

> Screams, cries and people running; their white faces like death masks; parents dragging children whose heads bobbed up and down in the water. . . . A wagon loaded to the breaking point lost a wheel and its passengers were dumped into the filthy water. . . . Bells were

ringing, the whistles in the mills were sounding a last warning, and steam engines opened their throttles for the last time. . . .

The Quinn house began to shudder as a flood wave smashed against it, lapping over the roof, hurling tons of debris. A shower of plaster and dust came down.

Gertrude was sobbing, "Papa! Papa! Papa!"

Her Aunt Abbie knelt, with her sleeping son in her arms, and said, "We'll all die together." She and the nurse prayed as the floor boards collapsed and the water spurted in.

Gertrude, never a passive child, was thrashing around in the water trying to grab something solid. She spotted an opening in one wall right under

the gables, and swung up. Her years of tomboy climbing had made her agile as a monkey. She pulled herself hand over hand along the rafters, wriggled through the hole, and landed on a mattress which had floated out of a bedroom window just below.

The impromptu raft kept tilting from side to side, so that she had to spring back and forth "catlike" to balance it. Once it slammed into a dead horse floating past on a tree, "bobbing up and down like a rocking-horse on a merry-go-round."

Soon the dead were human beings, some horribly mangled. The 6-year-old had never seen a dead person before; she prayed for help. It must have seemed as if her prayer had been answered

when a white house came floating along with a
man hanging onto the chimney. Gertrude hailed
him thankfully, and asked him to take her with
him. The man ignored her. She was so shaken by
this betrayal that she wanted to weep. But her
spunk flashed through and she yelled after him,
"You terrible man, I'll never help *you*."

Suddenly, across the water, she saw the old
Arcade building floating along, with at least twenty
people on its roof. Two of the women wore wide-
brimmed Leghorn hats with jouncy blue pom-poms.
When Gertrude shouted, she saw one man crawl
to the edge of the roof while his companions tried
to hold him back and keep him from going to her
rescue. She heard him ask them angrily, "Do you
think an angel from Heaven is coming down to
help her?"

After he had leaped into the churning water,
Gertrude watched with desperate attention, terrified
whenever his head went under. At last he bobbed
up again right beside her raft, and climbed on.
No angel could have looked more beautiful to her
than the dark-haired, square-faced rescuer with the
dripping moustache. He was a young mill worker
named Max McAchren—not that they had time to
introduce themselves just then.

McAchren was busy trying to pilot their raft
through the watery wreckage. Gertrude "put both
arms around his neck and held on." Either because
of his steering, or through blind luck, they were
out of the terrible mass surging toward the Stone

Bridge at the far end of Johnstown. Soon they were drifting along the edge of the water, toward the foot of a hillside. There a remarkable two-man rescue team—a tavern owner and his Negro porter—were at a window bordering the river, pulling victims to safety. Koch, the owner, leaned way out while the porter, George Skinner, gripped his legs. "Throw her to me," he shouted to Mc-Achren. People told Gertrude later she was thrown a distance of fifteen or twenty feet—and caught. McAchren was swept farther down-river, but he finally reached shore.

Gertrude's teeth were chattering with shock and cold. All her clothes had been torn off except her panty waist and panties. A third man wrapped her in a blanket and was carrying her up a hill when she heard voices yelling, "What have you got there?"

Even in her state of shock, she resented the gaping crowd, especially the man who came across the road. He peered at her so curiously that his long nose stuck almost into her face. Next, she was in a shabby, comfortable room already crowded with the owner's family, neighbors, and flood survivors. The wife, Mrs. Metz, took the shivering child on her lap and rocked her, while she sent people scurrying for red flannels and mason jars of hot water. After Gertrude was warm and dry, she tried gratefully to swallow the soup she was offered, but her throat was too tight with misery.

She was put to bed on a cot in a room with three other flood refugees, the Bowser sisters, twittery spinsters who kept running to the window all night. They talked in whispers, thinking the child was asleep, but she caught stray words—"frightful . . . terrible . . . ghastly . . ."

Finally she got up and went to look for herself. What she saw was "all water . . . over what was once our town . . . home and all we loved."

She had no idea whether her brother Vincent and her father and three sisters were alive or had drowned in that watery wreckage.

Like Gertrude's father, Frederick Krebs had been standing on the porch of his house at about four o'clock, smoking a cigar. He and his wife and their guest had spent several hours over the elaborate, many-course dinner. (Krebs was to remember wryly his joke: "Enjoy this; it may be a long time before we get another meal like it.") Several times during the meal he had looked out toward the great blast furnaces of the Gautier Wire Works, where he had dismissed the workmen that morning. The mills were more than a mile away, in the adjoining borough of Conemaugh, but he could see the stacks clearly. He had just gone back into the house when he heard an explosion. A neighbor yelled, "Krebs, there goes Gautier!" They saw the huge mill stacks "falling like tenpins." Metal shot into the air on great columns of steam, followed by billows of smoke.

Krebs didn't wait to see more. He ran into the den, turned off the gas fire, and yelled, "Gas explosion. Go to the attic." His wife grabbed a pet kitten and ran toward the stairs with their guest. Krebs raced back to the kitchen, where their maid sat holding a poultice to a swollen jaw. She had such a bad toothache she couldn't seem to imagine any worse trouble than that. Krebs had to bully and shove to get her upstairs.

Looking out the attic window he saw a church steeple from the Episcopal church across town hurtle down onto his front yard and land in a bed of petunias.

Of the sixteen churches in Johnstown, most were either badly damaged or in ruins. The Reverend Mr. Chapman's Methodist church and parsonage stood up best of all.

By four o'clock Friday afternoon, Mr. Chapman had given up trying to work on his sermon, with so many jittery women around. He took his granddaughter Nellie into the study and told her stories for a while. Then he went outside to see if the park looked less swampy. Their cousin, Mrs. Brinker, wanted to cross it to get home to her husband. As Mr. Chapman stood there, he saw a wild sight: a freight car careening down the sidewalk with a man standing on top of it. As it reached the corner by the parsonage, the man grabbed a tree branch and hauled himself onto the roof, shouting that the dam had broken.

He was the local agent of the Baltimore and

Ohio Railroad, who had heard a crash, climbed up on a freight car to see what was happening, and been carried off.

As soon as the Chapmans and the newcomer reached the attic, two more young men swung in through a window, using the same tree branch as a life line. Then a workman—they thought he was an Arab—bobbed in. He kept moaning in broken English, "Tronk! Tronk! Tree honner dollar." It sounded as if his life savings had been washed away in a trunk. But money seemed a trivial loss just then, to the others. With every crash, their hope dwindled for Mrs. Brinker's husband across the park. They could hear bookcases and china cabinets toppling over downstairs. The front porch was knocked off next, and uprooted houses kept scraping against the parsonage. The ten people huddled there in blankets were sure the house would collapse any second. It must have been an hour after the first crash when Mrs. Brinker asked Mr. Chapman in a trembling voice to look out and see if her house was still standing. "If it's not, don't tell me," she said.

In the twilight desolation, he saw one house left standing on the park, but it wasn't the Brinkers'. As he stood there silently, 7-year-old Nellie, beside him, piped up, "Yes, your house is gone, Mrs. Brinker. Your house is gone."

All of them were sure her husband must have gone down with it.

The German maid, no longer nervous, but full

of bustling kindness in an emergency, kept offering food from her cache to the grieving wife and relatives. (Thanks to her nervous insistence on carrying provisions to the attic, the Chapmans were almost the only family in town who had food that night.) At dawn she glanced out the window and jabbered excitedly in German. Nobody paid much attention. "Dere," she said, pointing. "Dere—I see Herr Brinker."

He was hobbling along over the wreckage in stockinged feet, with a red shawl around his shoulders. His wife shouted for joy, and kept clapping her hands as if applauding a miracle.

One of the young men ran down to help Brinker into the house, and searched around until he found a shovel. As Mr. Chapman said, so many homes and stores had been wrecked, "one could find almost anything."

When the men had shoveled a path through the knee-deep mud, the entire party started out, and met the leader of their church choir, who had come to see how they'd fared. He took them straight up to his little house on a hill, where twenty-four survivors had already found haven.

Nellie, who still had no real idea of the disaster, took a horrified look at people lying packed like sardines on the floor. She whispered to her grandmother, "If they haven't clean beds, we won't stay."

There were a few grown women who seemed as

unaware as Nellie of the desperate emergency. When rescuers raced into one house, they found a woman in an almost wrecked bedroom, primping in front of the mirror. Although the house was teetering, she wanted them to wait for her until she finished pinning up her front curls.

Another woman was seen going downstream standing on a plank. As she floated along, she was calmly taking one hairpin after another from between her teeth and putting up her hair as if she were expecting callers for tea any moment.

But the bravery shone far brighter than the bits of foolishness.

One survivor described how a little boy went by with his mother, on a roof. "Both were as calm as could be, and the boy was apparently trying to comfort the mother." A minute later they were hit by a new load of debris and killed. Twelve-year-old Elvie Duncan dove into the torrent and rescued her two younger sisters. A 14-year-old girl saved her brother's life, by holding him up after he broke his arm. A boy who had been known around town as a no-good turned into a hero. He ripped the slats from a hog pen, used two as paddles, and went into the very center of the churning water to save an old woman.

Sometimes there were astonishing, heaven-sent escapes. A father clung to a window sill with one hand, holding a child just above water, while his wife hung on beside him with the baby. Their strength was almost gone when a pair of large wooden steps shot out of nowhere and lodged under the exhausted man like a platform. He pulled his family aboard and they floated to safety.

A drowning woman was whirled past a tree, and a branch caught at her long hair and pulled her into shore.

A jaunty red-haired Irishman, Michael Ronesen, was walking down the street just after four o'clock when he heard a rumbling sound, glanced back, and had the bewildered impression he was being chased by a giant cloud. The wave caught him up, flinging him into the air. Each time he came down, falling timber knocked him under. Suddenly, on one upward fling, he was able to grab a lightning rod on a building that was still standing. He hung there for two hours until help came.

One man, being swept to what seemed a sure death, called to neighbors to tell his wife good-bye. Ten minutes later he was washed back, alive.

Some of the people who had bragged most loudly about their athletic prowess were among the first to die. A man who lived on the Flats near the Stone Bridge told neighbors noisily he was such a champion swimmer no flood could ever hurt *him*. They saw his body a half-hour later.

A 16-year-old boy orphaned by the flood, Victor Heiser, wrote about his experiences in his book *American Doctor's Odyssey*, after he became famous as a plague fighter all over the world. Remarking on the casual attitude of Johnstown's citizens to warnings, he said:

"The townspeople, like those who live in the shadow of Vesuvius, grew calloused to the possibility of danger. 'Some time,' they thought, 'that dam will give away, but it won't ever happen to us.' "

Victor's father had never expected it to happen either. His main thought, almost an obsession, was his son's education, and he drove the boy at a grinding pace. That Friday was no exception.

Day of Courage

Victor had known better than to ask his father if he could go out with his friends and ride logs downstream, or wade and splash and maybe take one of the horses for a canter through three feet of water. School vacation had just started, but Victor had to keep studying. Mr. Heiser, a veteran of the Civil War, had an almost Prussian passion for discipline, and he applied this to planning his son's schedule. In addition to regular school courses, the 16-year-old was being tutored in French and German, and this tutoring always continued through most of the summer. Victor had been brought up to obey like a soldier. The only time he had ever said no to his stern father's commands was when he was ordered to take violin lessons.

On the fatal day of the flood, Victor was studying in his bedroom when his father came in to tell him to go to the stable and take the carriage horses up to higher ground. The Heiser house was on Washington Street overlooking the swollen river. But the stable stood on a slope behind the house,

so that the overflow from the river hadn't reached there until midafternoon.

Victor was coming out of the stable leading the two horses when he happened to look at his watch. The time was 4:10. Just then, as he later wrote, "My ears were stunned by the most terrifying noise I had ever heard in my sixteen years of life. The dreadful roar was punctuated with a succession of tremendous crashes."

He saw his parents in an upstairs window; his father's arm shot up pointing at the roof of the stable, gesturing, "Get up there." Victor was so used to obeying he climbed up instantly. From the roof, he saw a wall of water roaring down the street, "A dark mass in which seethed houses, freight cars, trees and animals. As the wall struck

Washington Street broadside, my boyhood home
was crushed like an eggshell, and I saw it disappear."

He looked at his watch again. "I wanted to
know what time I was dying." It was 4:20 P.M.

The stable creaked and rocked, then rolled over
and over like a ball, while he scrambled to stay
on top. A neighbor's house rushed at him and he
grabbed hold and swung on. As the walls caved
in, another house came along. "I caught hold of
the eaves and swung dangling there. . . . For years
afterward, I was visited by recurring dreams in
which I lived over and over again that fearful
experience of hanging with my fingernails dug
deep into the water-softened shingles, knowing that
in the end I must let go."

He dropped and landed, by freak luck, on his
own stable roof again. Lying on his stomach, he
went bumping along in the surging flood. He saw
the Italian fruit dealer, Mussante, with his wife
and two children, racing along on what Victor
thought was their barn floor. All four Mussantes
were packing clothes into a steamer trunk, "ram-
ming them in as busily as if off for a holiday."
While Victor watched, their craft hit a mass of
debris, killing them instantly.

Victor was soon jammed between a church and
a brick building. He jumped aside as trees and
girders fell. When a freight car toppled down, he
thought that the end had come for sure. Instead,
the car slammed a hole through the brick wall

beyond, and the boy shot through into moving
water again. He saw a neighbor woman go by
astride a tar barrel. She was already covered with
tar, swaying and struggling.

Then he lost sight of her, as his roof raft
reached big Stone Bridge at the far end of Johnstown. The seven arch supports were already so
clogged that wreckage was piling up for a mile
behind, with hundreds of struggling victims caught
in the jam. The boy leaped off on a pile of debris
and joined a group of rescuers. While buildings
around them melted "like a lump of sugar," he
stood holding a clothes pole out like a fishing rod
over the grinding, heaving water, pulling in anybody who could grab it.

The flood, instead of quieting, was getting worse.
As the wave struck the mounting wreckage and the
steep embankment at the left of the bridge, most
of the water was flung back to wash again over
the ruined streets. Meanwhile, the second flood
wave, which had cut across town and joined Stony
Creek, was rebounding with more force than ever,
swollen with creek water. This created a kind of
sidewash that kept striking against the backwash,
so that houses were tossed back and forth, and
spun like wooden tops.

The house of lawyer Horace Rose, bordering
Stony Creek, was hurtled across town three times,
and spun dizzily in this whirlpool. The wave hit
soon after Rose had passed candy tied on a broom

to the child next door. He had just passed a tin cup of coffee to the child's mother, a trickier balancing feat than the candy, when they heard a crash. The woman put down the cup on the window sill and said, "What is it?"

She was dead before she ever knew the answer, along with the gay little daughter who had reached for Rose's candy. Both of them had been buried under crashing masonry.

John Dibert, the neighbor down the street whom Rose had talked to that very noon about a flood-reform committee, was killed a minute later, with most of his family, as their house fell.

The Rose's house was crushed like a matchbox. Rose later said, "There was a crash, a sensation of falling, a consciousness that I was in the water, and all was dark. A moment later, I felt a sense of excruciating pain."

His right arm and ribs were smashed, his collar bone was broken, and the pressure on his chest was so violent that he thought he was being crushed to death. The voice of his youngest son, Percy, cut through the haze of pain, urging him to get up on a higher spot. With the boy's help, Rose crawled onto a fragment of slate roof. He thought his wife and daughter must be dead because he had seen them sucked into the torrent. Just then, their heads came to the surface again. He saw his son Winter dive in, and heard him say, "Ma, hold onto me and I can save you."

Winter was a husky 20-year-old, but his rescue

work proceeded with agonizing slowness, as the
flood water pounded at them. His injured father
lay twenty feet away, frantic because he couldn't
do anything. Suddenly a young man seemed to
shoot up out of the debris at Rose's side. Rose
begged him to help Winter save the women, and
explained that his right arm and side were useless.
The stranger rushed over and pulled Mrs. Rose
free, while Winter lifted his sister to safety and
rescued an old lady going past on a shutter.

The Roses' oldest son, Horace, had vanished
during the first crash. By now, 14-year-old Percy
had been swept off too. The others crawled onto
a more solid roof that floated by, and started on
their wild, perilous ride up and down Stony Creek,
across town to the Little Conemaugh, and back
again. The Unique Skating Rink, where the Rose
boys had often cut gliding figure eights, sailed past
them, like an ocean-going liner. A soda fountain
floated by, then a church organ. Their roof raft
passed St. John's Church, which had caught fire
and was blazing fiercely. Rose always remembered
how weird he felt, drifting on water past fire. The
big bell of the Lutheran Church struck five
o'clock, the bronze hammer pounding out each
slow stroke. To the Roses, it tolled like a funeral
knell.

But an hour later, as it struck six, a rescuer was
leading them across a mound of wreckage, into the
attic of Dr. Swan's house. It was one of the few
havens that held fast.

Anybody in Johnstown would have sworn that the handsome new 4-story brick hotel, the Hulbert House, was the strongest building in town. Certainly stonecutter Joseph Smith thought it was the safest place to leave his young wife and three children. He had taken them from their small frame house down by the river that noon, and installed them in the comfortable hotel lobby. Then, feeling satisfied that they were safe from any flood, the big man went back to chiseling a granite tombstone. A day later, he had his entire family to bury.

Of the fifty-five people in the Hulbert, only eight escaped. More lives were lost there than in any other building in town, as the brick walls toppled.

The owner, Mr. Benford, heard the screech of whistles, and asked his son to see where the fire was. The son, at a window, yelled that he could see a cloud of dust. It looked to him as if Prospect Hill had caved in. His father took one glance and knew what had happened. He ran to the kitchen to tell the maids, then started upstairs to yell a warning. Some of the guests followed him up. But others, including Joseph Smith's wife and children, sat in the lobby, still trusting blindly that the brick walls would hold. As the flood wave hit head-on and the building collapsed, they were buried under tons of bricks.

The wooden mansard roof swirled off like a hat and landed across the street. One of the hotel guests, a Mr. Hartley of Philadelphia, who had been flung into the water, reported:

> Catching hold of something I managed to pull myself up on the roof . . . Down on the extreme edge, I espied the proprietor, Mr. Benford. He was nearly exhausted . . . I managed to creep down to where he was hanging on. I tried to pull him up but found that I was utterly powerless. Mr. Benford was nearly as weak as myself. We did not give up, however, and in a few minutes he managed to crawl up on the roof.
>
> Crouching and shivering on another part of the roof were two girls, one a chambermaid of the hotel and the other a clerk in the store next to it. . . . An hour later they were rescued, more dead than alive.

A survivor at the American House sat alone that night on the hotel's roof, shivering and forlorn. Suddenly a large dark blob came out of the water and thumped toward him, huge reddish eyes glistening. When it brayed, the man was so startled he nearly fell off. But a mule was better company than nothing. Until daylight he and the animal huddled together. And the man later said he was "grateful for the companionship and warmth."

Some of the flimsy wooden hotels stood up astonishingly well under the battering of the flood. Before the Merchants Hotel finally collapsed, later that night, a New Yorker named Klein, who had been staying there, helped haul sixty people out of the flood. One of the men Klein saved was swimming past with a table balanced on his head. On it sat his wife and child.

A block away, the Keystone Hotel moved across the street and whammed against its longtime competitor, the Fritz Hotel. The owner of the Fritz ran to rescue his rival as the Keystone crashed.

Often, frail wooden houses survived and floated to safety, while the heavy stone ones toppled. The municipal building went down and so did most of the stores along Main Street.

The Union Street brick schoolhouse held up, and two hundred survivors reached it. The most unusual arrival there was a Mrs. Mangus, who swam in through a window with a baby in a sling. She and her husband had been whirling downstream in the attic of their house when the flood waters suddenly tossed a naked baby in through the window. They had no idea whose it was.

When Mrs. Mangus swam into the schoolhouse, she was holding the baby's sling by her teeth, much as a mother cat carries a kitten. She unwrapped the child to make sure it was still alive, and began massaging its cold little legs. Just then, a weeping woman walked past her, took one look, and gasped, "My baby! My baby!"

Over on Vine Street, Mrs. Leudie Masterton had sat at the window all morning and early afternoon, watching the flood. She was a newcomer in Johnstown: "I had rather enjoyed it as it was my first flood experience." She and her husband were leaning out the window talking to a neighbor when the wave hit, "in a cloud of the blackest smoke I ever saw." When the smoke cleared, they saw that the neighbor's house had been thrown upside down. Masterton picked up his small daughter, and he and his wife ran to the attic. In the noise and confusion, they didn't even realize their house was afloat until Leudie looked out and saw they "were just opposite the Market Street schoolhouse."

The house kept whirling like a dervish, somehow collecting telegraph wires that wrapped it round and round like a bale, and held it upright.

"When we had recovered ourselves a little, we began to see what we could do. We succeeded in getting twenty-seven people into our attic." As Leudie Masterton helped in one exhausted, badly bruised victim, she cried out, "Why, it's our mailman!" He had been carried down from Conemaugh Borough.

The young housewife opened trunks and closets and yanked out the winter underwear she had just stored away in mothballs. After Leudie had every "poor drenched creature" in dry, warm clothes, one of the women gave birth to a baby boy. When the child yelled lustily, the thankful group in the attic agreed with the new mother that he should be christened Moses.

He was one of the half-dozen children born during that night of terror. Two of them were christened "Flood."

The Night in Alma Hall

All day Friday, the Reverend David Beale of the Presbyterian Church had been stalling about taking up the carpet in the parlor. He kept insisting that the water would go down any minute. His wife disagreed. At four o'clock she won the argument. The Beales' young sons, who were ten and twelve, helped their father roll up the rug, while he protested it was "contrary to my own judgment." They had just finished when a man who belonged to Mr. Beale's church came in with his two sisters. Beale heard a sound "like that of an approaching railroad train" and glanced out the window to see a mountain of water rolling down.

He shouted, "Upstairs! Upstairs, everyone."

His daughter grabbed up the canary in its cage. The boys took their wire-haired terrier, Guess. Mr. Beale picked up the family Bible, and shooed the others up the stairs as the water surged in the front door. The hall hatrack floated out and shoved into his back, prodding him on his way. He had just reached the second floor when a man came through a window as if shot from a catapult. The newcomer had been washed down from Woodvale, three miles away, on the roof of his wrecked house.

The Beales' house was already shuddering, as water slammed against the walls and buildings collapsed all around it.

In the attic, the Reverend Mr. Beale opened the Bible and read aloud from the Forty-sixth Psalm to the group that expected death any moment.

> *God is our refuge and strength, a very present help in trouble.*
>
> *Therefore will not we fear, though the earth be removed, and though the mountains be carried into the midst of the sea.*
>
> *Though the waters thereof roar and be troubled, though the mountains shake with the swelling thereof. . . .*

Then his 10-year-old son recited the Twenty-third Psalm:

> *The Lord is my shepherd; I shall not want. . . .*

Everybody was quieter, and the group gathered in the attic all looked to the minister trustingly. He knew that he must lead his flock somewhere. But where?

Every time he looked out the window, he could see more houses in ruins. Out in the grinding, roaring flood water, he saw a dozen familiar faces go by. Two little children, alone and almost naked, were holding hands and clinging to a roof as it passed—too far away to reach. But as the mound of debris piled up outside the parsonage, Beale glimpsed his old friend, Captain Alec Hart. The Captain, along with his wife, sister, and two little boys, was struggling in the watery mass. The minister and the other men in the attic formed a human chain and hauled the Harts, one by one, up through the window. Fifteen people were now in one shaky attic, with the floor already sagging ominously.

As Beale later wrote in his book, *Through the Johnstown Flood*, Captain Hart was a heartening ally to have around, because he was cool-headed and practical. The two men consulted in undertones on the next move. The parsonage couldn't hold up much longer, and the solidest building they could see was Alma Hall, standing four stories high amidst the wreckage of Main Street. Captain Hart thought they could walk over the debris and reach the Hall.

But the shifting wreckage was a hazardous bridge to safety. Twenty feet of water covered the streets. The flood backwash from the clogged Stone Bridge was settling like a filthy lake over the devastated town.

The men decided to take a chance while it was still light enough to see their way. They let down a rope, and Captain Hart went out first to steady the women and children as they slid down. Mr. Beale waited until the last. He was just leaving the attic when his sons, below, began pleading for their dog. "Oh, please, please, Father, let us take Guess along."

Guess was whimpering, as if begging too. His master carried him down, and the terrier had no sooner landed on the debris than "true to doggish nature, he and a neighbor's cur engaged in an earnest and free fight for supremacy."

The fifteen people crawling over smashed houses, and jumping from one mound to another, must have envied Guess his four-footed passage.

One of the women in their party slipped on a plank and "fell into the watery chasm so that we could see nothing but her hair floating on the surface."

They managed to yank her up, and got to Alma Hall just as darkness closed down. As soon as the women and children were safely inside, Beale and Captain Hart went back over the treacherous route to haul out several more struggling victims and escort them to the refuge.

Lawyer James Walters, who had an office in Alma Hall, was at his home on Walnut Street, a mile away, when the flood hit. His family was carried off in one direction; Walters was swept down the street, through an alley, and tossed right into his own office on the second floor of the Hall. At first he thought he must be delirious and imagining things.

Dr. Matthews had been knocked down by falling

timbers but in spite of his smashed ribs, he was carrying on singlehanded, trying to tend the injured on all three floors.

Of the 264 people who reached Alma Hall, many were in such a state of shock or fear that they were incapable of helping. There were women sobbing, children crying, injured victims moaning or sitting in numb silence in the dark.

The dozen most responsible men went into the hallway and held a quick meeting on the stairs, to set up a plan of action. They elected James Walters as director to take overall charge. The

Reverend Mr. Beale, Captain Hart, and Dr. Matthews would each be director of a floor. Matches were forbidden, because of the danger of explosion from a leaky gas main. The sick and injured, and the women and children, were given the best places. Even then, they shivered in wet rags on the floor.

All night, water lapped against the building, and a contractor who had taken refuge there declared loudly, over and over, "This place will never hold up."

Engineer John Fulton, who had written the report on the dam for Cambria Iron Works, managed to reach Alma Hall with his wife and all but one daughter. The fact that he had been right in pointing out the urgent need for repairs was no comfort that tragic night. He was convinced that his missing daughter, who had been downtown when the flood struck, must be dead. When she crawled in a window of the Hall, there was a tearfully happy reunion.

Frank Traut of Woodvale was one of the battered late arrivals, after Miss Fulton. When the first wave bore down, he had swung from a roof to a telephone pole, and as it snapped off, he had vaulted onto a log and ridden it two miles along the murderous flood path.

Dr. Matthews had used up his makeshift bandages long before Traut staggered in. There were no drugs to ease pain. The injured were trying hard to be stoic, but bewildered small children kept crying, begging for something to eat or "a drink of water." Several men took turns holding a pitcher up to the eaves, to get rain water, so the youngest refugees might have a sip.

Nobody slept. Dr. Matthews kept going the rounds, and even the most seriously injured survivors hung onto life with his help. As for Beale, one survivor said of him: "Throughout that dreadful night in Alma Hall, he was incessant in his attentions. . . . By his kind, consoling words, by his calmness and self-control, by his fervent prayers, he made it possible for us to endure the horrors of that night."

The fire that broke out at dusk, in the debris piled up at Stone Bridge, brought the most awful horror of all.

The Fire Rages

Almost three thousand men, women, and children had been swept down to the wreckage piled thirty feet high at Stone Bridge. Many of them had crawled out before dusk. But about a thousand were still trapped in the ruins when the fire started. Petroleum had spilled from an overturned freight car. Live coals from a stove in one of the wrecked houses fell on the oil-soaked timbers, and the blaze shot up and began eating its way through the tightly packed mass of debris that covered at least sixty acres. A cargo of lime fed the flames until they burned like a monstrous funeral pyre.

The people of Johnstown may have been careless or lazily indifferent to the threatened danger from the dam. But once the danger was there, at its fiercest peak, many of them showed incredible courage—literally under fire. In the nightmare from dusk to dawn, at the Stone Bridge, they hauled hundreds of people from the flames.

Rescuers armed with axes, knives, or just their own raw, bleeding hands, worked in teams to free the trapped victims, while the fire ate its way relentlessly. The bales of barbed wire from the Gautier Wire Works had wound all through the wreckage, binding helpless survivors to every kind of debris. The pressure of flood water packed these masses even tighter.

A 19-year-old girl, Rose Clark, was caught by the weirdest trap of all. For an hour, she had struggled to pull herself free. When rescuers reached her, she explained calmly that something had caught her ankle under water and was holding it like a steel band. One of the men risked his life to dive down and discover the grim answer: A dead man's hand was clutching the girl in a death grip. Another member of the team said, "She was the coolest person I saw that night at the bridge, though in the greatest danger, as the fire was gradually creeping up to where she was held. I several times thought we would be compelled to cut off the one foot that was still held rather than let her be burnt alive."

Not once did the girl cry out, or scream at the men to hurry. By the time they pulled her free, the fire was scorching their backs.

Another girl in the path of the fire refused to be taken out of the wreckage of her house. "Not till you get my father." She insisted he must be alive in the water underneath the house. The rescue crew thought she was hysterical, but to humor her they yanked up more timbers, and found she was right. Her father had been caught between two walls and was suspended there. They

carried him out, unconscious but alive, while the flames crackled around them.

A 12-year-old boy and his younger sister showed a courage that moved grown men to tears. They were the children of John Fronheiser, a superintendent of the Cambria Iron Works. He had gone home early that day to be with his family in case of trouble. Their big house crashed as the wave smashed down Main Street toward the Stone Bridge. Mrs. Fronheiser and one daughter were drowned instantly. Her husband caught the baby and handed it in through a window at the Cambria Clubhouse. Then he struggled back to find that his other children were both trapped in the wreckage.

Meanwhile the fire was eating its way closer and closer. Ten-year-old Dorothy called, "Let me go, Papa, and save Jacob. My leg is pinned down by timbers and I think it's broken."

Twelve-year-old Jacob begged his father to escape before the fire caught them all. "You can't save me. Both my feet are caught."

An Army captain headed the team that helped Fronheiser free his two brave children. All that night Dorothy lay on a neighbor's attic floor, with her broken leg unset, while water sloshed below. One of her rescuers described how she managed to smile and blow a kiss to her grieving father, assuring him, "I'm all right, Papa."

The Army captain and other Civil War veterans who had joined the rescuers at the Stone Bridge said the scenes during the fire were more horrible than anything they had seen on the battlefronts.

William Tice, the owner of a drugstore, was carried toward the bridge on a roof. Sailing at about fifteen miles an hour, he saw a woman floating down even faster, singing:

> *Jesus, lover of my soul*
> *Let me to Thy Bosom fly*
> *While the raging billows roll*
> *While the tempest still is high.*

When his own raft drifted to shore near the fire, he jumped. And, as Mr. Tice reported later, ". . . a mill man caught hold of my hand and assisted me to land; he was terribly excited and could not speak."

Tice stayed there long enough to help pull in two more survivors. Then he went up on the embankment above Stone Bridge and looked down at the blazing wreckage. ". . . At last I could endure it no longer . . . I climbed the hillside where I could see the church on fire close to the house where I had left my wife, but I could not see the house and did not know she was safe."

The church he had seen blazing was the handsome big Roman Catholic Church, St. John's. It had been uprooted and thrown against the house next door, where the cook was baking a cake. As the kitchen walls fell, the fire from the stove licked out, spread, and consumed the church and a convent. The steeple crashed with a shower of red-gold sparks, at ten o'clock. The priest and his household had escaped. Long before that, a brave priest from another parish, Father Trautwein, had rushed to the fire at the bridge, to join the rescue crews. He told a New York *Sun* reporter later:

A thousand persons were struggling in the ruins and imploring for God's sake to release them. Frantic husbands and fathers stood at the edge of the furnace that was slowly heating to a cherry red. . .

> Everyone was anxious to save his own rela-
> tives, and raved . . . until the air trembled . . .

Most of the relatives were so hysterical that
instead of helping the rescuers, they would scream
at Father Trautwein and other volunteers, "Go to
that place. Go here, go there. Get her out. Save
him." No matter which spot the rescue team
tackled, the relatives of some other victim would
rage and rant. Each naturally wanted his own
family saved first.

In spite of this chaos, the teams kept their heads
and worked steadily, ahead of the fire. Father
Trautwein said, "Every effort was made to save
every person who was accessible, and we have the
satisfaction of knowing that fully two hundred were
spared."

At least three hundred more died there in the
fire.

Editor George Gibbs, marooned in the *Tribune*
office, went on writing his sorrowful, moving eye-
witness account:

> Wild shrieks for help . . . The houses, piled
> mountain high, took fire and burned with all
> the fury of the hell you read about. . . . People
> watched the flame, and questioned one an-
> other. It's going down; it's blazing up again;
> it's coming this way! Calls from roof to roof,
> "What's burning now?" and answers that in
> the awful stillness succeeding the first wild
> hours had an awful sound. "Who are you?

Who's with you?" and so, in the way that
rumors fly . . . hearts that had hoped sank in
despair, while hearts that had feared and
quailed for loved ones thanked God that they
were saved.

Providence certainly seemed to have a hand in
saving a young mother, Mrs. Schultz, and her
small children. They were in a house being swept
along by the torrent, straight toward the fire. Mrs.
Schultz didn't panic. She used her lovely soprano
voice, trained in her church choir, to sing hymns
to the children. Suddenly there was a great jolt
that threw them to the floor. When they got up,
they saw an incredible sight. A huge tree had
rammed through the side wall, impaling the house
to the riverbank, halting it just short of the blaze.

Charles Phipps floated from the fire at St.
John's Church almost to the fire at the bridge.
Earlier that day he had been teasing his dog for
being afraid of the water in the cellar. But the
loyal dog had stuck with his master all through
the flood, jumping from house to crashing house
till they landed with fourteen other refugees on a
solid piece of debris, a safe distance from Stone
Bridge. Phipps said:

We managed to get hold of some floating
canvas and made a little tent under which we
huddled together to keep off some of the
rain. . . . My dog had followed me through it

all, and as several of us had no shoes on, we made him lie down at our feet to keep them warm.

Whenever Phipps and his companions dozed off from exhaustion, there would be another muffled cry from the swampy wreckage beneath their refuge. Each time they heard a cry for help the men would crawl down to find one or more people nearly suffocated, their heads just above water. Altogether, they saved nineteen people. And the faithful dog went on serving as a heating pad for the half-frozen survivors.

While the flood wave had been trying to push through the clogged arches of Stone Bridge, one prong had hurled itself futilely at the steep embankment to the left. Because of this, and the acres of wreckage that were slowing up the flow of the water, the flood wave was losing some of its driving force. But it still had enough power to plunge down on Millville and Prospect, the small boroughs to the right of the bridge, before attacking Cambria City, just below Johnstown.

Five hundred flimsy frame houses belonging to workmen were swallowed up. The lower plant of the Cambria Iron Company toppled, as did every other building except a brewery. Mayor O'Neill, who a few hours before had politely discouraged the two would-be Paul Reveres, saw his wife and baby drowned. Many people who had shrugged off the same men's warnings with,

"We've heard that before," were corpses floating downstream.

The flood, having lost its smashing force at last, no longer leaped the banks. It simply carried its last victims, dead or alive, down the swollen river. In the villages along the Little Conemaugh, the rescues went on through the night, as watchers paced the banks with lanterns to provide a beacon of hope.

Rescues Down-river

A trainman stranded four miles below Johnstown, at Sang Hollow, said the whole village turned out in a massive rescue operation. "Not just men, but the women, stood on the banks with ropes."

A boy they hauled in gasped, "Watch for my mother," before he lost consciousness. A woman came along held up by a board under each arm, and a rescuer alerted by her son went into action. He held onto a telegraph pole with one hand, swung out over the churning flood water, and grabbed the woman. Two brakemen helped carry her up the embankment, to the cabin of the stalled train. When they had poured hot coffee between her blue lips, and she and her son were reunited, somebody mentioned what an effective life preserver she had improvised by using the two boards as supports. The woman looked absolutely blank; she had no recollection of where or how she had got them.

Watchers saw one little girl in a white dress, kneeling on a piece of timber with her hands clasped, praying. She drifted close enough for them to run along the bank shouting encouragement. Ropes couldn't reach her, but everybody was so struck by the little girl's courage that they kept hoping she would be rescued farther down-river. When they heard her body had been found in a large clump of willows at the next bend, even the men wept. The willows and a great sycamore tree that hung over the water were traps responsible for more than a hundred deaths. But thirty were saved at the Sang Hollow telegraph tower, where the operator and his helpers leaned out the window and grabbed people out of the swollen torrent four feet below.

At Bolivar, the next village down, the river suddenly rose from six to forty feet just after dusk. Rescuers stood on the town's two bridges, lowering ropes into the boiling water. But even when the struggling victims saw the ropes, the swift current either carried them along so quickly that they couldn't grab one or the rope was torn from their exhausted hands.

After these heartbreaking misses, one boy finally caught hold of the rope, was wrenched away, then caught it again under his left arm. He was hauled up, swinging perilously, and flung against the iron support, but he still held on. As he was pulled over the side of the bridge, bleeding and tattered but safe, the crowd of watchers cheered.

The boy told a rescuer that his name was Edward Hessler and he was sixteen years old.

With my father I was spending the day at
my grandfather's house in Cambria City. We
looked out of the door and saw persons running. My father told us to never mind, as the
waters would not rise further. But soon we
saw houses swept away, and we ran to the
floor above. . . . We were at last forced to the
top one. In my fright I jumped on the bed.
It was an old-fashioned one with heavy posts.
The water kept rising and my bed soon was
afloat. Gradually it was lifted up. The air in
the room grew close and the house was moving. Still the bed kept rising and pressed the
ceiling. At last the posts were pushed against
the plaster. It yielded and a section of the
roof gave way. I found myself on the roof
being carried down stream. . . . I did not see
my father. My grandfather was in a tree but
he must have been drowned. [The boy then
named seven other people, relatives or friends,
he had seen drown.] . . . All along the line
were people who were trying to save us, but
they could do nothing and only a few were
caught.

A rescuer told about seeing a young man with
an older and younger woman, perhaps his mother
and sister. "At the upper bridge a rope was thrown
to them which they failed to catch. He was then
seen to instruct the women how to catch the rope
that was lowered from the second bridge. Down came
the raft with a rush. The brave man stood with his
arms around his two companions. As they swept

under the bridge he seized the rope. He was jerked violently away from the women, who failed to get a hold. Seeing that they could not be rescued, he dropped the rope and fell back on the raft, which floated on."

The young man finally managed to grab at a tree, and pull their raft in. Just then, a section of the bridge collapsed and floated downstream, striking the tree and snapping it off. The young man and the two women he had come so near saving were thrown into the water and drowned.

A mother who went past with her two small children shook her head and refused the rope, because she wouldn't desert her babies. She couldn't have carried them both and held onto the rope. One of the few happy bits of news that night came from downstream at Cokesville: The mother and her children had been saved. A 5-month-old baby in its crib floated seventy miles on a floor, and was hauled out just above Pittsburgh.

In Johnstown, a man carried his sick wife on his back to the Union Street schoolhouse. There, jammed in with two hundred other refugees, he nursed her through the endless night. At daybreak, as the sun came up, he rushed outside shouting, "It's morning! It's morning!"

Editor George Gibbs of the *Tribune* wrote:

> Little by little the streets came into sight.
> People were stirring. Men who were first to

leave the wreck on which they had passed the weary hours were shouting everywhere. Rafts were out. Hearts beat again. Hope rose with the sun. The birds sang their most cheerful songs. Then came the real awakening. . . . People went over miles of debris, at the risk of life and limb, to find no sign of their homes.

Where the houses had stood was bare ground. . . . The Cambria Iron Mills were wrecked. The Gautier and Woodvale Mills were gone and so was every business house in town—or, if the building remained, the merchant moved among us a tramp like the rest.

Freight cars, carried long distances, stood in the streets. Here was a big hotel, filled with people when the water came, nothing left of it—even the cellar to be dug over again. . . .

Survivors were moving, but they knew not whither. Over and under the wrecks they went, in and out of the ruins—hoping, dreading . . . The bridges were gone and the rivers divided us. In parts of the town there was still a waste of waters.

The water had gone down enough for rescuers to spot people still stranded near the smoldering drifts. A young Cambria executive organized a flotilla of four boats that went through the watery debris taking off survivors. They picked up a cheerful young woman holding a baby in her left

arm; her right arm hung limply, broken. The baby cooed and held out its grimy hands to the rescue team, and the mother assured the men that her child was fine. "And so's Grandpa," she added. Then she let out a lusty holler, "Hey, Grandpa!"

An old man came scrambling up over a half-submerged roof and leaped into the boat. "Gentlemen," he said, "have you a chew of tobacco?"

At Alma Hall, one man had crawled out at the first glint of daybreak. He came back with a sodden box of crackers and a bunch of bananas, which he divided among the children.

The Reverend Mr. Beale and his family left the Hall and walked over mounds of wreckage—"piled up 15 or 20 feet high"—until they reached the hill. They found more than three thousand survivors already there. Mr. Beale wrote, "Every one of that vast crowd was either injured in some form or had been bereft of kin or loved ones. Their agony was so intense as to be oppressive and held them in the grip of a vise, so that no one was seen to shed a tear."

The farmhouses there were so jammed that the Beales slogged on, over the swampy roads, till they reached the home of friends in Daisytown.

Citizens who lived in Johnstown proper had often made scornful remarks about Daisytown's being so far away, so inconvenient, up such a steep hill. Who would want to live *there*? they said.

Now every house in Daisytown was a haven for exhausted survivors: children even slept on cupboard shelves and on pianos. Mr. Beale left his family there and went right back to the muddy desolation to help wherever he could.

His friend Captain Alec Hart told him that Johnstown's chief of police had lost his wife and five of his six children, and was seriously ill himself, from shock and exposure. The sheriff was missing, and at least half the members of the City Council. Everywhere they looked, houses and stores lay in ruins, with their contents spilled out and exposed to any thief. Survivors wandered dazed through this chaos. Captain Hart and a steel manufacturer, Tom Moxham, were organizing a Citizens' Committee to take charge and keep order. But most of the men were so exhausted they wouldn't be able to stand guard around the clock to prevent looting.

Beale hailed a boy he knew and gave him all the change in his pocket, along with a scribbled message to Governor James A. Beaver in Harrisburg, asking that the National Guard be sent at once. The boy promised to get the message through as soon as he reached a telegraph tower that was still operating.

The wires were down, the railroad tracks were torn up, the bridges into Johnstown were all swept away. The few houses still standing were filled with mud and even corpses. And families cut

apart by the catastrophe went crawling through
the ruins looking frantically for each other, and
asking everybody along the way, "Have you
seen . . . ?"

Six-year-old Gertrude Quinn was still too numb
with shock to tell her name. Several people
thought she might be the "little tow-headed Quinn
girl," but her hair was so muddy and matted, her
face so scratched and bruised, that they couldn't
be sure.

The twittery Bowser sisters who had shared the bedroom with her were standing on the porch the next morning when they saw Gertrude's Aunt Barbara Foster go by. Mrs. Foster and her husband and six children had escaped to Bedford Street Hill before their house was hit. Now she was heading for Green Hill because it was nearest the Quinns'. If they were still alive, she thought that was where they would be.

The Bowser girls called to her, "Oh, Mrs. Foster, would you come in here and see if this child is your niece?"

It was Gertrude, in a borrowed calico dress, and for once she was muted. Her aunt hugged her thankfully. "You stay right here," she said briskly, "and I'll find your family and bring them all back."

She was talking with more confidence then she felt. But ten minutes later she found Gertrude's father and three sisters in the yard of a farmhouse where they had spent the night. James Quinn was washing his gaunt face with pump water, and at first he refused to believe the good news Mrs. Foster brought. As soon as he had found that Gertrude and the others weren't following him, he had sent a neighbor on up the hill with the little girls, and had gone back to collect his missing whitehead. But as he turned the corner, he had seen their house carried off in the flood.

When Mrs. Foster convinced him that Gertrude was safe, he said, "If she's really alive, I'll never punish her again."

He began running down the hill, the soapy lather still on his face, with Helen and Rosemary trotting behind.

The sight of them brought Gertrude to life. She made a flying leap from the porch steps and landed in her father's arms. "We both cried," she wrote later.

Rosemary was sobbing, "My poor little sister, oh, my poor little sister, we'll never leave you again."

Gertrude had soon recovered her spirit so completely that she was complaining about having been given shoes that didn't match. How could she walk in such terrible-looking things? Her father didn't scold her; he picked her up and carried her.

Her adored brother Vincent was still missing. They learned later that he had been helping his Uncle Louis move goods from his confectionery store to a warehouse on the hill, when the flood struck. His uncle had tried to persuade him to stay there on high ground, but Vincent refused. "I must help save the little girls."

He was a few blocks from home when the wave caught him. "A man in a third-story window saw Vincent's straw hat come to the surface, spin around, float away, and disappear."

Vincent's body was found three days later in the backyard of his grandfather's lawyer.

Gertrude's grandmother was found lying unconscious by her son Louis on a mound of debris,

the day after the flood. Her scalp and neck were
so torn that the scars lasted all the rest of her
life. "She always wore frilly little caps with ribbons,
to hide the marks," Gertrude remembered. Her
grandfather wasn't even hurt. Their store and their
houses were lost, but as a family they were much
luckier than most.

That Saturday afternoon a man in rags came
down a street piled with the wreckage of houses,
including his own. But his face was radiant as he
called to a friend, "I've found my son—alive!"

One Hundred Reporters

The first news of the flood to reach the outside world went clicking over the wire from Sang Hollow on Friday at dusk. Robert Pitcairn, superintendent of the Pennsylvania Railroad's Mountain Division, had been on his way to inspect tracks blocked by landslides. He arrived in Sang Hollow just as the flood wave surged past, and a survivor gave him part of the horrifying story. A repair crew that had tried to reach tracks near Johnstown supplied hearsay accounts. The bodies in the churning river below the telegraph tower carried grisly proof. Pitcairn had the operator tap out a message to the *Commercial–Gazette* in Pittsburgh, the nearest large city, eighty miles away:

JOHNSTOWN ANNIHILATED. THOUSANDS OF LIVES LOST. URGE THAT MAYOR OF PITTSBURGH CALL MEETING AT ONCE TO ORGANIZE RELIEF MEASURES.

The *Gazette* passed along the message to the mayor, but the publishers knew a spectacular scoop when they saw one.

By 9:00 P.M. the newspaper had a special train hurtling toward the flood area—a locomotive with one car. The reporters in it were hanging on for dear life, around the curves. They had to get out at Bolivar, twenty miles below Johnstown, because the tracks beyond were washed out. It was midnight, and they could find only one horse for hire, so they drew lots to see who would ride ahead to New Florence, to secure a telegraph line. The losers slogged through the mud on foot.

Like most of the villages anywhere near the river, New Florence was buzzing, even at 3:00 A.M., with news of the disaster. Within an hour, the reporters had gathered enough fragmentary accounts to flash their first stories.

The *Commercial-Gazette* hit the streets soon after dawn on Saturday with splash headlines:

EXTRA! A STUPENDOUS CALAMITY. THE CONE-
MAUGH VALLEY SCRAPED BARE AND THE TOWN
OF JOHNSTOWN WIPED OUT BY AN OVERWHELM-
ING DELUGE FROM A MOUNTAIN LAKE

Long before then, other Pittsburgh papers had chartered special trains. A newsman who became a legend during the next week was one of the first to leave. He was Colonel Connolly, the head of Associated Press in western Pennsylvania—a big, genial, silver-tongued man who could write as well as he talked. He and his crack telegrapher, Harry Orr, and a free-lance reporter named Wetmore, trudged on foot from Bolivar. Finally Connolly, with the help of a fifty-dollar bill, persuaded a farmer to drive them over the mountain in his wagon. After a jouncy 6-hour ride, the man let them out three miles below Johnstown, at the bank of the Conemaugh River.

In the early morning light, they saw dozens of bodies lying in the muddy wreckage.

The three men went slipping through the mud until Connolly stepped into a hole and twisted his ankle so badly it swelled like a balloon. Harry Orr and Wetmore helped the big man up to a farmhouse on the hillside, and told him he would have to give up and let them take over. To Connolly, those were fighting words, but for the moment he sat back meekly.

His companions walked on till they got within a mile of Johnstown, and spotted a lineman up on a railroad telegraph pole. He had a pocketsize Morse transmitter and had just cut in on the line to report to the Pennsylvania Railroad's office in Pittsburgh.

Wetmore shouted up, "We're reporters. Could you send a message for us?"

The repairman refused. He said the line was for railroad business. Wetmore hung on like a bulldog at the foot of the pole, yelling and pleading. Finally, the harried lineman tapped in and got permission from his superior to take a message. "But only a few words," he said.

Wetmore scribbled on a scrap of damp paper,

fastened it to a long stick, and thrust it up to the man perched at the top of the pole. It went to the Associated Press in Pittsburgh:

OVER 2,000 DEAD
JOHNSTOWN APPEALS TO THE
NATION FOR FOOD AND SHELTER
FOR OTHER THOUSANDS WHO ARE
HOMELESS AND STARVING

That done, Wetmore and Orr walked on and set up Associated Press headquarters in an abandoned gristmill. They had barely arrived there when Colonel Connolly appeared, supported on each side by a farmer who had been dragooned into serving as his crutches. Connolly lay down on his stomach on a board and, using one end of the board as a desk, began writing. Orr and Wetmore serving, literally, as his leg men kept rushing out to interview survivors and explore the ruins.

By late afternoon, Western Union had three wires in operation. One was reserved for official dispatches to the state capitol at Harrisburg. One served the military (Army and National Guard). The third wire belonged exclusively to AP, thanks to Connolly's fast talking. He had managed to convince the authorities his firm represented most of the major papers.

Once the line was theirs, telegrapher Orr sat right down and began tapping out the dispatches

Connolly had already written.

What they didn't know was that the general manager of the Associated Press, William Smith, had been on the express stalled at East Conemaugh when the flood struck. Smith had stood on a hillside and watched, stunned, while the wave engulfed Johnstown. Then he clambered up a mountain till he came to a driver of an ore wagon, near a mine. Smith waved a fist full of dollar bills, and the driver agreed to take him over the rain-swept mountains to Ebensburg, almost twenty miles away. They arrived at 11:00 P.M. on Friday, and Smith found that the Western Union line to the east was still open. He got through to the Philadelphia bureau of AP, and for two straight hours filed his story. Then he signed off so that he could return to Johnstown and take charge.

It took him until Sunday afternoon to get there, and he found Colonel Connolly and his assistants already working at top speed. Part of their headquarters had been taken over as a temporary morgue, so they were surrounded by coffins and corpses. Other reporters who had managed to get into the flood area by then were snatching what sleep they could. Then at dawn they rushed out to hunt around for their day's food. The first relief trains reached a point below Johnstown early on Sunday, and some food was given out to survivors, but there wasn't enough to go around. Reporters bought their own—a few eggs here, bread and sausage there—from farmers' wives. The

New York *Tribune* man told of a colleague who, while interviewing survivors huddled on a hillside, carried a huge basket of bread over his arm, and distributed it wherever he went. When several cows wandered into sight, men and women rushed to milk them, and get milk for their children.

In comparison with the townspeoples' suffering, Connolly considered his own hardships trivial: a throbbing, puffy ankle, no sleep at all, and a diet of crackers and muddy coffee. His only concern was to get out dispatches on the most sensational peacetime disaster in Pennsylvania's history. The major papers were giving their entire front pages to the flood, and for the first several days, the AP accounts provided the only on-the-spot coverage. The simplest, strongest opening description of Johnstown was Connolly's for AP: "The wreckage covered the water thicker than the houses stood in the town before. It was no longer a flood of water. It was a town afloat."

By Monday night, four more Western Union wires were open, and eighty or ninety reporters had reached the "Valley of Death," with still more to follow. After working seventy-two hours without a break, Connolly collapsed. Associated Press Manager William Smith took him back to Pittsburgh on a relief train that had brought in supplies. But by then, Connolly's marathon stint had made him a legend with other newsmen.

Among the new AP men who came in to replace Connolly was a strange-looking specimen, a

young New Yorker who had been covering a
formal dinner of city officials when he got the
word from his editor to leave instantly for Johnstown. He set off wearing a tall silk hat, snowy
starched evening shirt, and cutaway coat. After
three days of traveling by roundabout ways to the
flood area—the last miles on foot—he arrived battered and splattered, looking like a scarecrow that
had known better days. He cut the tails off his
dress suit, rolled up his trousers, and got down to
work.

The New York *Sun* men had been shunted off
on the longest detour, up to Erie in western Pennsylvania and down again. One of them wrote
somberly, "Nobody who has been here an hour
would think anything too awful to be possible."

The first fire brigade from Pittsburgh—two
horse-drawn engines—arrived on Sunday. Firemen
had their hoses trained on the tightly packed,
burning sixty acres of wreckage, but as the *Sun*
said, "In the immensity of the disaster, their feeble
efforts seem like those of boys with squirt guns
dampening a bonfire."

Nobody knew how many dead were still at
Stone Bridge, or anywhere else, for that matter.
In those first nightmare days, so many bodies were
turning up that there were piles of empty coffins
every few hundred yards, waiting to be filled.
Many of the dead had to be burned in community
graves in the first frantic days. The citizens' committee in charge of burials, headed by Mr. Beale

and Mr. Chapman, had set up eight temporary morgues, one in the Presbyterian Church with boards laid across the pews. Survivors spent days trudging from one to the other, searching. Sixteen-year-old Victor Heiser found the body of his mother after six days of looking, but he never found a trace of his father.

Eight thousand telegrams from frantic relatives and friends piled up at the Citizens' Relief Head-quarters, but nobody had time to open them.

Often the first news of dead relatives came from the casualty lists published in newspapers. Reporters did an extraordinary job of getting around. They went from borough to borough and from morgue to morgue, to collect the names of newly identified dead people and to get survivors' stories. All the bridges were gone, and most of the horses had been drowned. Towns were such muddy ruins that even people who had lived in them for years couldn't find a familiar street.

It is no wonder that newsmens' first estimates of the total casualties were high: from 5,000 to 10,000. The best informed officials in Johnstown believed the estimate to be correct. It was a week before most reporters settled on a figure closer to the truth: approximately 2,500. (The final official count, weary weeks later, was 2,209 dead. Of these, 967 bodies were never found.)

Newsmen noted one poignant detail: survivors never used the words "drowned" or "burned to death." They said "so-and-so has gone down."

Or "he went down the river."

Women walked barefoot along the street, with wet shawls over tattered clothes, and some murmured the same word over and over. Their faces were cut, bruised, and sickly yellow from lack of sleep. Sometimes they carried pitiful little bundles, all they had managed to salvage. People who had been only casual acquaintances before the flood would meet and embrace each other mutely.

"A peculiar silence hangs over Johnstown," wrote one reporter. "Nobody speaks loud or calls out. There is a sort of suppressed horror. . . ."

Main Street was a sea of mud piled with debris: a tangled mass of furniture, bedding, stoves, dead horses, a baby's crib. The telegraph poles that were still standing leaned drunkenly. A man from *Harper's Weekly* spotted a wagon wheel sitting on a grand piano, with three crystal chandeliers on top. A woman's chiffon veil streamed from a half-open trunk in the street. A clothing-store dummy stood with wooden hand outstretched, beckoning. Strips of clothing, even a feather boa, hung from timbers. An uprooted steel track lay twisted into a perfect letter *S*. A locomotive lay on its back with its wheels in the air, like a discarded toy model. Through the smashed wall of the First National Bank, the vault sat in plain view, still holding Cambria's Saturday payroll.

Blue-uniformed National Guardsmen were stationed every few hundred yards with bayonets attached to their guns. Volunteer policemen, all Johnstown citizens, were armed with baseball bats found in the wreckage of a sporting-goods store.

The contents of houses and stores were strewn around as if they had burst out of overstuffed suitcases. But there was surprisingly little looting, in spite of the lurid accounts in early news stories. A typical headline in a Philadelphia paper was:

ROBBERS OF BODIES LYNCHED

FOUR HEARTLESS THIEVES DRIVEN HEADLONG TO DEATH WHILE OTHERS FIND SPEEDY JUSTICE AT END OF ROPE

Johnstown citizens were enraged by these published accounts, with good reason. There were enough legitimate horrors, they felt, without inventing new ones. (The man who came closest to being strung up was a grocer who set up a stand and started selling potatoes at five dollars a bushel.)

Soon responsible reporters were wiring their city editors to beware of all "ghoul and lynching stories." But they complained in print about the ignorant boorishness of some of the new tin-starred deputies who delighted in showing their authority. All newsmen had to carry passes signed by the state's Adjutant General Hastings, who had come from Harrisburg to help organize emergency relief, or by the chairman of the Citizens' Committee. But one swaggering new sheriff refused to honor any passes not signed exclusively by himself.

At first the only way to get from borough to borough was by little skiff ferries, and this too required special passes. The boats were often so crowded that newsmen had to wait for hours to get aboard. But they wrote with compassion of a boatman who worked day and night and wouldn't take a cent of fare from valley people crossing and recrossing the river while trying to find missing relatives.

The survivor who seemed to move the reporters most, judging by the long, touching accounts they wrote, was "a pale, pretty little woman" named Mrs. Fenn. The afternoon of the flood, her husband had come home from his store and volunteered to do the family marketing in the rain. When the wave hit, he was killed at once, on the street.

Mrs. Fenn collected her six children in an upstairs room and explained cheerily that Papa would soon come for them in a boat. When they were driven to the attic, she said they must not be frightened because God would look after them.

When the water was up to the smaller children's necks, one of the little girls said calmly that she thought it would be better to go outdoors. Their mother put them out the window, one by one, on pieces of floating timber. The 4-year-old went last, saying, "Don't worry, Mama. I'm not afraid."

When the house crashed, Mrs. Fenn was thrown into the torrent. Hours later, when she recovered consciousness, she was in a tree surrounded by water. Her clothes had been torn off. A man floated a tin of biscuits to her on Saturday afternoon. Then a woman passed along a skirt, and rescuers reached her in a boat. By Wednesday, she had found the bodies of two of her children and had given up hope for the others. She told the New York *Tribune* reporter, "Now they're all gone and I am so tired."

Hearing and writing stories like this, day after day, made the newsmen savagely bitter about the members of the South Fork Hunting and Fishing Club. With the exception of the Pittsburgh *Commercial-Gazette*, which tried to whitewash the whole affair, the newspapers made it clear that the owners had been warned repeatedly that the dam was dangerous, and had refused to make repairs. The *Times* said:

> To have put the dam in excellent condition
> would not have cost $5,000. Carelessness, which
> in the minds of an intelligent coroner's jury
> might be termed criminal—was the sole cause
> of the deluge. . . . The cause of the calamity,
> it is admitted by the President of the Club . . .
> was the weakness of the dam alone, and the
> tremendous pressure of water behind it.

The same paper reported drily that the club-house and cottages were unharmed. And from the puddle that had been the lake workmen carried off baskets full of fish they had found in the mud —the same game fish that club members had protected at the cost of human lives.

New stories also reflected the valley's resentment at Governor Beaver, who was conspicuously absent. As reporters noted, he *finally* found time to come to Johnstown—eight days after the flood.

Luckily the state's Adjutant General Hastings was doing a good job. He arrived in a lumber jacket and high boots, slept on the floor of a shack until his tent arrived, and proceeded briskly to organize the cleaning up of the ruins. He encouraged all Cambria plants to call back their men at once, to dig out machinery, and to salvage whatever they could. (Of 1,300 men who had been on the Gautier payroll the week before, 487 reported for work.) The task of clearing Johnstown itself was much too massive for exhausted survivors. Within a week, Hastings, with the help of relief

committees, had imported from other towns
thousands of workmen and derricks, cranes, and
teams of horses. He also did his best to keep out
the ghoulish sightseers, the souvenir hunters (who
snatched anything from family silver to a cherished
baby picture of a child now dead), and the camera
bugs who swarmed over the ruins. All of them
took pictures of the Schultz house showing the tree
that had rammed through it, stopping it just short
of the fire. Hundreds even lined up at relief commissaries for a free lunch. Hastings ordered all
photographers not on newspaper staffs to join work
crews for a brief stint of clearing away the mess
of slime and corpses. Then he told them to get
out of Johnstown, and most of them did.

He never ordered the newsmen to leave, but
neither did he do much to make their job easier.
They complained they were enduring almost as
many hardships as the survivors. Every farmhouse
and village within fifteen miles had taken in so
many homeless refugees that they had no rooms
to rent to reporters. Soldiers of the National
Guard's 14th Regiment, and workmen clearing the
ruins, had tents to live in. But here again, newsmen were left out in the cold. Most of them still
snatched a few hours sleep wherever they could,
with straw for blankets. They used coffin lids or
shovel bottoms to write on. The *Times* man described how the luckier ones could luxuriate at
night in a haymow in a barn. For background
lullaby, he said, they had "the tuneful piping of

hundreds of mice, the snorting of cattle, the nocturnal dancing of dissipated rats."

A dapper Philadelphia colleague arrived a week late, to do feature stories, and sent the veteran reporters into wild roars of laughter when he asked innocently, "Where's a restaurant?... Where can I hire a horse and carriage?... Where can I buy a clean white shirt?"

This was young Richard Harding Davis of the Philadelphia *Press*, who always strolled around elegantly in an English lounge suit, a yellow ulster with green stripes, fawn gloves, and a Malacca cane. In Johnstown, he added high rubber boots to this outfit, and sent back stories that helped make his byline famous. He was to become the most glamorous foreign correspondent in newspaper history, and a novelist who lived the adventures he wrote about.

Wandering through the flood ruins, he found the one-cell city jail still locked. In it was the body of a prisoner who had been arrested for drunkenness on Memorial Day. The man was due to be released just as the flood wave struck. Davis described how the trapped prisoner had looped his overcoat over the top cross-bars, to support him like a hammock, as the water crawled up and up.

John McLaurin of the Harrisburg *Telegraph* was another newsman with a lively eye for color. He told about the bride and groom who had just been declared man and wife in a ceremony at the bride's parents' home when the water roared over the town. The whole wedding party spent the night in the attic. When they picked their way through the rubble the next day, the bride was holding up her ivory satin train daintily.

McLaurin was amused that a half-dozen women who had been marooned in a barn refused to come out because their clothes had been completely torn off. Rescuers had to bring blankets and solemnly swear to turn their backs while the ladies covered themselves.

At Relief Headquarters, McLaurin reported

hearing a flouncy young woman in line tell a
clerk she must have, at once, "Two dresses, two
sets of underwear, two pairs of shoes, and two
hats—*new goods only*." The clerk stared at her. "If
you could wait," he said, "we're expecting a con-
signment of diamond rings and gold watches."

The always hungry newsmen reported indignantly
that some people would go through a food line
as often as six times, undetected, and leave with
five hams and a dozen bags of flour, while others
got nothing. The New York *Herald* said relief
workers tossed out coffee, canned food, and loaves
of bread, "as they would unload bricks, throwing
them without looking where they went."

Even after the relief depots were much better
organized, it didn't seem to occur to officials that
reporters couldn't work on empty stomachs.

Most of the newsmen had rushed to Johnstown
without warm clothing. While they were there,
they were perpetually wet, cold, exhausted, and
frustrated by all the red tape. And they were
continually delayed in their job by the difficulty
of getting from one place to another. Even in
normal times, Johnstown and its nine sister boroughs and offshoot villages would have been a
confusing place for newcomers to cover. But with
all landmarks washed away, and so much debris
lying everywhere, it took most of a day to walk to
a spot three miles away. In view of all these
difficulties the stories they got seem all the more
remarkable.

A reporter told how the church bells in Mineral Point rang wildly as the steeple crashed. He asked a survivor when the village had received its first warning and noted the terse answer, "When the houses started coming down the valley."

One old man explained solemnly that the wave advanced "faster than a horse could trot." Several women said they thought Judgment Day had come, because of the black clouds of smoke and the thunderous noise.

Reporters caught the poignant small touches: a teapot still sitting on the shelf of a wrecked house; a cross-stitched sampler, *There's No Place Like Home*, hanging on a smashed wall; the grand piano sitting on the riverbank, with a small boy in rags playing it absorbedly; the rows of dead laid out, and a searcher in the long line finding a familiar face and standing by the body weeping, while the guard said, "Move along. Move along."

Day and night, reporters crawled over the perilous debris on their rounds. Two were badly injured in collapsing wreckage, and had to be taken home. The others went on filing millions of words in a telegraph office right above the horrors and stench at Stone Bridge.

All over the country, readers bought every edition for flood news, and stood in crowds in front of newspaper offices to read the headlines posted on bulletin boards.

Most survivors in Johnstown resented the newsmen; their attitude was, "We're the sufferers.

You're the intruders."

But it was the newsmen who told their tragic stories in moving detail, and started the generous flow of millions of dollars in money, food, and clothes—everything from candles to carloads of lumber.

Not just Americans, but people all over the world, responded.

Help Pours In

Even before the first relief trains arrived, help was coming from the hills.

Some of the farmers who drove down just after dawn for Saturday market day hadn't even known about the flood until they saw thousands of survivors sitting on the wet slopes above Johnstown. They promptly handed out everything in their wagons that they had brought to sell at market— butter and cheese, gallon cans of milk, sides of beef and pork, and vegetables. Then they headed their horses for home to collect all the spare blankets and clothes they could find.

In the mountain villages, the courthouse bell rang urgently, summoning people to donate whatever they could. Men formed volunteer work groups to leave at once. Women stood in doorways with armloads of clothing, as a wagon collected supplies. In Altoona, thirty-nine miles away, doctors gathered surgical instruments and medicine, and set off for the disaster area. All day, wagon trains came over the mountains in a rolling stream.

In Pittsburgh, citizens jammed into City Hall

Saturday for a one o'clock meeting called by the mayor. Members of the South Fork Hunting and Fishing Club were conspicuously absent. All of them seemed to have gone into hiding to avoid reporters. But other Pittsburghers who crowded in clamoring to help raised fifty thousand dollars that afternoon.

The Pennsylvania Railroad had put empty cars on a siding, marked JOHNSTOWN FLOOD RELIEF, and local merchants piled them high with supplies. By 4:30 that afternoon, the first relief train left for Johnstown, with twenty cars, one full of coffins. Seventy-five members of the Pittsburgh committee, plus several doctors and police officers, went along. The railroad's repairmen had been working all night to lay new tracks. By dawn on Sunday, when the supplies reached the edge of Johnstown, some weary survivors waiting near the tracks called out, "God thank you."

A member of the Pittsburgh Relief Committee said:

> The anxious people crowded around the cars begging for something to carry to their homeless families. It was only after forming a line from the train to the temporary store-houses that the supplies could be unloaded and taken to a place where a proper distribution could be made. Within a few hours after the arrival of the train the yellow ribbon [the badge worn by relief volunteers] was seen in all parts of the devastated valley. Every man had come to work and help the afflicted. . . .

Of the half-dozen citizens' committees already
functioning in Johnstown, two went into action as
fast as trains were unloaded. The group in charge
of distribution set up commissaries and supply
depots in the few buildings left standing, including
the railroad station.

The Sanitation Corps headed by the heroic Dr.
Matthews, under the direction of the state's health
officer, started at once to disinfect the whole
valley. They had to search through the debris to
find containers—coffeepots, washtubs, dishpans—to
hold the first supplies of carbolic acid. Soon more
than two hundred workmen, under twenty-two
inspectors, were pouring tons of lime and nitric
acid on the wreckage and in the cellar holes
where buildings had stood. Even the houses that
were still intact were covered with filth inside;
every room, every sewer outlet, every street and
alley had to be disinfected. The sunny, warm
weather made the problem of infection even more
urgent. The danger of a typhoid epidemic hung
in the foul-smelling air.

Six local doctors had been drowned. Cambria's
little cottage hospital had room for only those
patients in the most critical condition. These
included the injured who had to have an arm or
leg amputated, and the most serious cases of
pneumonia, caused by exposure. One emergency
hospital was set up in a "lager beer hall," with
forty-one cots. Blankets were hung down the middle of the room to separate the mens' and womens'

wards. The floral decorations left over from a dance, chains of pink paper roses, still hung from the ceiling.

Eighty more patients lay on the floor of a loft over a livery stable. The Sisters of Charity who had lived in the convent beside St. Johns Church were nursing in every hospital.

At dusk on Tuesday, a small, gray-haired woman wearing rubber boots and a muddy uniform with an arm band appeared at the entrance of Adjutant General Hastings' tent office. "I'm Clara Barton of the Red Cross," she announced. Later she said that General Hastings seemed surprised, but that "he couldn't have been more kind." Considering that this 68-year-old woman was the founder of the American Red Cross, the heroine of Civil War battlefields, and world-famous, it's understandable that General Hastings rallied quickly. The very next morning he gave her the workmen she wanted. Three hours later, under Miss Barton's calm supervision, they had a field kitchen set up on Prospect Hill, and were handing out hot soup. By the next day, there were nine Red Cross tent hospitals. The largest held forty patients; the smallest had ten cots apiece.

Miss Barton had heard about the flood on Saturday in New York. She had organized supplies and a starter unit of five assistants, including a woman doctor who had grown up in Johnstown. Two weeks later, she had a staff of fifty. Altogether, she distributed a half-million dollars' worth

of aid to 25,000 people. Her desk was an up-ended
dry-goods box; she never left it except to snatch
meals and a few hours of sleep, and to make
the rounds of the hospitals. One reporter said she
had added "a little white apron and a nurses'
cap" to the gray uniform that came to her boot
tops. Her olive-skinned face was "plain, but a face
full of tenderness mingled with determination."

The Red Cross disaster unit from Philadelphia,
which had set up its own tent hospital, sometimes
thought Miss Barton was entirely too full of
determination. Their unit was performing most of
the emergency operations, and the hard-working
young surgeons felt they could function very well
without a woman boss. But when they wanted
mattresses for a second hospital tent for contagious
diseases, they pocketed their resentment and went
to her to ask, Please, might they have what they
needed from the mountain of supplies she kept a
watchful eye on.

Chapters all over the country were rushing
contributions. Sawmills in the midwest and on
the Pacific Coast had sent, through the Red
Cross, carloads of lumber. General Hastings went
to Miss Barton humbly, to ask if he could have
enough to build a "guest house" in a hurry for
Governor Beaver, who had finally agreed to come
to the disaster area. Both Hastings and Miss
Barton lived and worked in tents, but the Governor had to have something more splendid for his
one-day stay. Miss Barton obliged with the lumber,

but she put most of it to better use later: a warehouse to hold contributions ranging from furniture to pans; three Red Cross hostelries with bedrooms, a sitting-room, and one central dining hall that served meals for fifteen to twenty-five cents.

If many citizens had resented the Governor's staying away, they were even more bitter about what he did when he came eight days after the flood. He put Johnstown under state rule (in effect, martial law, although he denied this). The authority of citizens' committees was canceled, and Hastings was in control for the state. People complained that the state militiamen were more bother than good, that they ate like horses and spent too much of their time trying to flirt with young girls. But George Gibbs of the *Tribune* said:

> The soldiers came, their rows of white tents standing where the Second Ward used to be, and the boys were ready for any hardship if only they could serve, guard and protect us ... Bless the soldiers, with their human hearts!

Pittsburgh and Philadelphia contributed more in relief, in money and in supplies than the state gave officially—more than a half million dollars apiece. New York, where General Sherman was in charge of fund-raising, ranked as the third highest contributor among cities.

A Baptist church in backwoods Georgia sent 55 cents. Buffalo Bill played a flood benefit in Paris and cabled $2,000. Top prize fighters put on an exhibition match. Theater people, from the great Edwin Booth on down, gave benefit performances. Queen Victoria sent her sympathy, but an English drug firm sent $2,500 worth of disinfectant. The Sultan of Turkey handed over $876.57.

School children collected money to buy new textbooks and to repair schools. One class sent money asking that it be used for little Mrs. Fenn, who had lost her husband and six children, and was living in a Johnstown hostel. The young senders explained in a note that their contribution was to buy a pretty rug for Mrs. Fenn's room.

The Pittsburgh Masons sent one of the first and best-planned donations: a hundred complete outfits for men, women, and children—from underwear to coats and shoes. They also sent hundreds of sandwiches and containers of cooked food.

The Brotherhood of Carpenters and Mechanics sent members to help. On Wednesday there was the heartening sound of carpenters hammering. Army engineers were putting up two pontoon bridges sent by the Secretary of War. This was the first cool, cloudy day, and it brought some relief from the smells.

All drinking water had to be boiled to kill germs. But nobody could light a gas fire, because there was still danger of natural gas mains exploding. And even the kitchens that hadn't been wrecked were waiting to be disinfected. The Reverend Henry Chapman described how oats sprouted in the mud in the parsonage sink. For the first two weeks, huge iron cooking pots hung on poles over bonfires, as in some vast military encampment.

The worst danger of pollution was the four square miles of wreckage at the Stone Bridge. Even after the fires were out, workmen could only hack loose the edges of the tangled debris held together with miles of barbed wire.

The Sanitation Corps and clean-up committees finally decided to dynamite the area. The demolition expert sent from Pittsburgh, Arthur Kirk, was a cocky little man who stood with his feet apart, like Napoleon, and told newsmen he was the "Prince of Dynamiters." One wrote, "He personally superintends the preparation of all blasts, and when ready emits a peculiar cry, more like a wail than a warning. Then he surveys the atmosphere with the air of a major general and yells 'Fire!' The yell often terrifies spectators more than the explosion."

At first, the New York *Sun* explained, Kirk only used 6-pound charges, for fear of damaging the Stone Bridge.

> Even with this . . . the whole structure shakes as though with an earthquake at every discharge.

> The dynamite is placed in holes drilled in logs matted into the surface of the raft, and its effect being downward, the greatest force of the explosion is upon the mass of stuff beneath the water. At the same time each charge sent up into the air 100 feet or more a fountain of dirt, stones, and blackened logs.

But Kirk wasn't satisfied with this small-scale (to him) method of clearing the debris. He soon set off a 450-pound charge that broke windows and made walls quiver all through the valley. People said bitterly he'd blow up whatever the flood had left whole.

The next week the state dismissed Kirk and hired a Major Phillips to clear the river channels. He caused even more uproar than Kirk by exploding charges late at night. These charges were so powerful that many people were thrown out of bed. Even several newly repaired water mains were broken. Residents whose nerves were already raw from all they had survived tried to have him arrested. It's possible that Pittsburgh officials were putting pressure on the state government to let the work proceed as fast as possible, because the city's water supply was threatened by pollution too, from this tributary of the Allegheny. Phillips went right ahead, disregarding local protests, and by June 26th he had cleared a channel from the Stone Bridge to the Point. A month later, both rivers, Little Conemaugh and Stony Creek, were flowing freely down the valley.

The vast typhoid epidemic every doctor feared had been short circuited. Forty people died of fever, instead of the hundreds or even thousands some health experts had predicted.

Long before the rivers were cleaned out, and less than a week after the flood, enough wreckage had been removed from Main Street to clear a path down the middle, for wagons to pass. The whole town was digging out. "The work has progressed so far that the outline of some of the old streets could be faintly traced, and citizens were going about hunting up their lots."

A workman digging under a charred house was astonished when a cat crawled out. It had most of its hair singed off, but was able to lick its rescuer's hand in gratitude. Two chickens, alive and clucking, were found under a barn, as was a dog who just managed to wag its tail. Workmen heard a voice coming from an attic, and hurriedly cleared a path to reach the survivor. They found a parrot squawking furiously, "A devil of a time. A devil of a time."

Six days after the fatal Friday, a survivor searching wearily at the Stone Bridge for the bodies of his missing family saw a small girl crawling out from the ruins. She had been there all week. When the man learned that her parents were dead, he immediately adopted her, and the two comforted each other.

A sign in front of the house serving as a temporary post office asked citizens to come in and register, so that there would be an official record of survivors. People stood in long lines waiting a turn, and compared losses in quiet voices. Those who had never found members of their families still went the rounds of the morgues, searching through the piles of jewelry or clothing found on mangled, unidentified bodies already buried. Most of the tagged descriptions on these were pitifully brief: "Watch-chain and plain gold ring marked H.B. to M.S.Mc. on female 20 to 25 years of age. . . . White dress and brown bib of a girl about 6 months old, dark hair. . . ."

The final casualty lists included 395 children under the age of 10. One hundred families had been wiped out entirely. Four hundred and seventy children had lost one parent; ninety-nine were orphans. Some of them went to live with relatives. Two women from the Children's Aid Society set up a bureau in Johnstown to find homes for the others. They were so swamped with telegrams and letters from every state, offering to adopt flood orphans, that they soon announced, "There are not enough orphans to go around."

Hetty Ogle's son found the bodies of his mother and sister in the ruins of the Western Union office. A wire went off to every branch of the telegraph company:

H. M. OGLE DIED IN THE JOHNSTOWN FLOOD

Cyrus Elder, the once-debonair counsel of Cambria, who had been on his way home when his rowboat overturned near the park, never saw his wife and daughter again. He put personal grief aside to work on the town's emergency finance committee, and to help speed the rebuilding of Cambria's plants. The flood wiped out at least fifteen hundred homes and caused more than seventeen million dollars' worth of damage. Almost one-third of that consisted in Cambria's losses in factories and machinery.

Gertrude Quinn was in the crowd that watched the reopening of the first mill that summer. There was no roof on it yet. As the flames from the heating furnaces leaped high, and the first red-hot steel bars came out of the rollers, the crowd cheered. With Cambria back in operation—even one small part of it—Johnstown felt more normal than at any time since the flood.

Of the eight relief commissaries, seven were already closed. By mid-July only widows and elderly or sick people were receiving cash relief allotments. Everybody who was able to work had a job. Some townspeople who had lost everything they possessed turned the tables neatly on the scavenger souvenir hunters pawing through the ruins. They set up stalls and sold bits of junk, even muddy corset covers, as "flood relics," for fancy prices.

Housing was still the biggest problem. Quite a few people had gone to stay with relatives in other towns, but some of them returned when several hundred prefabricated houses bought with relief funds went up. The first one-room, easily assembled wooden houses were called "Oklahomas" because so many homesteaders had used them when they settled in that state. Relief officials soon realized these were too flimsy and ordered 400 "Hughes" houses. These had four rooms and two stories. By then a joke was going around Johnstown: A man living in an "Oklahoma" wanted to sneeze, so his wife grabbed the nearest wall and held it steady, "because an Oklahoma is nothing to sneeze at."

People chuckled about the buried treasure found on Main Street. A man killed a sheep and buried the offal under the foundation of what had been a furniture store. While he was digging, he came across a butter crock crammed with gold pieces, $6,500 worth. The place had originally been owned by a Scotsman, long since dead, and people said that if he had been saving for a rainy day the flood was certainly it.

Soon after the middle of June, Adjutant General Hastings called a meeting of local merchants and businessmen, and said he was going to erect temporary stores and offices on all four sides of the park. The names of men who applied for space in the buildings were put in a box for a lottery drawing, and on the Fourth of July, a small boy proudly drew out the slips determining who got what location.

Merchants who wanted to build their own stores were offered free lumber; one even set up shop in a piano crate. The *Tribune* reflected the local excitement when ice cream, the first luxury since the flood, appeared in one of these makeshift stores. Soon Decker's Ice Cream Parlor reopened formally. A piano tuner came to town on July 9th. In August, a pet shop unveiled a noisy array of Cuban parrots, canaries, and mocking birds. A salt-water taffy machine in a store window drew crowds, but the real sensation was the demonstration of an "Edison earphone phonograph" on Main Street.

The Pennsylvania Railroad was rebuilding its roundhouse in East Conemaugh and its marshaling yards were bigger than ever.

In October, the state turned over all authority to the citizens, who had earned it. Under the efficient guidance of General Hastings, they had done a magnificent job of putting their town back together. Schools were open; steel plants were working around the clock to catch up on orders; Main Street had the raw-wood look of a frontier town in spots, but it was bustling.

Clara Barton left that same month, because the place was getting entirely too comfortable and normal. The intrepid 68-year-old was off to hunt new disasters. Grateful citizens presented her with a gold pin and locket. Miss Barton, when she arrived in Washington, told newsmen, "Enterprising, industrious, and hopeful, the new Johnstown, phoenix-like, rose from its ruins, more beautiful than the old."

But the 2,209 dead citizens couldn't rise phoenix-like from the ashes, and thousands of shattered lives would never be whole again.

The South Fork Hunting and Fishing clubhouse and the cottages sat empty, their windows staring blankly at what had been the lake. Signs were still nailed to the trees there.

PRIVATE PROPERTY

ALL TRESPASSERS FOUND HUNTING OR FISHING
ON THESE GROUNDS WILL BE PROSECUTED TO THE
FULL EXTENT OF THE LAW

The Coroner's inquest in Cambria County, five weeks after the flood, returned a verdict signed by the six members of the jury impanelled to investigate. The last paragraph said:

> We further find, from the testimony and what we saw on the ground, that there was not sufficient water weir, nor was the dam constructed sufficiently strong nor of the proper material to withstand the overflow; and hence we find that the owners of said dam were culpable in not making it as secure as it should have been, especially in view of the fact that a population of many thousands were in the valley below; and we hold that the owners are responsible for the fearful loss of life and property resulting from the breaking of the dam.

Most members of the club were still hiding from reporters, and the New York *World* accused them of "a conspiracy of silence."

In the first edition of the Johnstown *Tribune* to appear after the Flood, there was a bitter editorial headlined, "A Day Long To Be Remembered." It went on to say, "The thousands who were lost two weeks ago were struck as with bolts of lightning . . . and gave up their lives for no cause. . . . A few years ago along came the Pittsburgh club men, in all their spotlessness and glory, who wanted an exclusive resort where they might idle away the summer days. Costly, picturesque houses were built on its shores, a big hotel was erected, and though all seemed lovely . . . a rat caught in a trap and placed in a bucket of water would not be more helpless than we were." The editorial pointed out that "all the penalty [is] on the heads of the innocent."

A reporter from Philadelphia, trying to interview the elusive owners in Pittsburgh, said, "No one will admit his membership in the club. . . . They are awaiting legal action which will probably be taken against them. . . ."

In view of all that, it is astonishing that there are no records of legal suits by survivors; none of the wealthy members were ever brought to court.

The only one who ever appeared in South Fork after the flood was the club's president, Colonel Elias Unger. With grim courage, he went on living, like a hermit, in the house he had built near the dam, above the town that had reason to hate him. When he walked along the slope around the reservoir, he must often have relived that terrible moment when twenty million tons of water smashed through the dam wall, and went plunging down on the people of Johnstown.

Johnstown: Free from Floods

The people in the valley towns had been united by disaster, and they wanted to stay that way. That fall eight of the ten boroughs voted to incorporate as the city of Johnstown. Under one central government, they could work together to repair flood damage and to finance it. By then, many citizens were saying that the flood would never have happened in the first place if the boroughs had joined forces and put pressure on the club owners to make them repair the dam.

Lawyer Horace Rose was the first mayor of the newly incorporated city. All his sons had turned up alive and his own injuries had healed, but he had not forgotten the plan he had discussed on the morning of the flood—to widen and deepen the river channels. In the three years of his administration, the city spent $75,000 on this program. The soil and rock removed from the two rivers was used to fill in and raise the level of Johnstown an average of five feet and to build up riverbanks, which were then fortified by concrete.

Everybody thought that completed the job. Even Mayor Rose, a staunch fighter for flood control, was satisfied. He announced that the river channel was cleared and "the grades of the streets have been raised above flood line."

There were still some costly nuisance floods during spring rains. But once again the valley was so booming with prosperity that nobody thought much about it. And with the dam empty, they couldn't see any reason to worry.

Twenty-four years after the flood, the state passed a law prohibiting construction of large dams without state approval and frequent inspection.

World War I erupted the next year, and brought an even bigger flow of orders to the valley's steel mills. During the next ten years, Bethlehem Steel bought up all of Cambria Iron, and added still more plants. By 1930 Johnstown and its suburbs had a population of 100,000.

And in March of 1936 disaster rushed down from the hills again, during the spring thaw. This time, there was no mountainous wave of dam water, but the two swollen rivers washed over Johnstown in one afternoon. Twelve people were drowned, seventy-seven buildings were wrecked, and two thousand homes were damaged. Warning whistles rang wildly at 2:45 P.M. on March 17. A rumor that "the dam has burst" heightened the panic. There were four large dams within twenty miles of Johnstown. Nobody was sure *which* dam, but the phrase itself terrified anybody brought up in that city. To heighten the panic, a wildly irresponsible ham radio operator broadcast a frightening description of how the city was to be wiped out. People ran frantically for the hills, and stayed there for hours. By the time they realized that the rumors were false, one woman had died of a heart attack, four other people had died of shock, and hundreds were ill.

The flood water went down just after midnight,

and many people were able to go back to their homes the next day. But the damage to the city was estimated at $41,000,000.

Once more, the Red Cross rushed help, and newspapers sent reporters scurrying to the scene. It wasn't a disaster on the monstrous scale of 1889, but it jolted the city and state into demanding federal action. That same week, army engineers arrived to make the first surveys on flood control. The actual work started in 1938, and followed the lines of Johnstown's own original plan under Mayor Rose. This time, almost three million cubic yards of earth and rock were removed, and the built-up riverbanks were reinforced with concrete for miles. The cost was about $8,000,000. The city and state paid some of this; federal funds supplied the rest.

By this time both federal and state governments were more aware of the importance of taking proper flood-control measures. Heavy floods in the Mississippi Valley and other river valleys caused Congress to adopt the Flood Control Act of 1936. In 1938, $376,700,000 was set aside for a five-year program of building and keeping up reservoirs, levees, and flood walls.

In 1943, Johnstown was free from flood at last.

Each spring, after heavy rains, the swollen rivers go rushing past the city—harmlessly.

In the early 1960s the dam still sat moldering in the hills, and the shabby old clubhouse was called Clement's Hotel. A week or so after the

1889 flood, the owners of the clubhouse announced that they had considered turning the place into a home for flood orphans, but decided it "wouldn't be suitable for that purpose." Perhaps they realized that children who had just lost their parents might not want to live beside the dam that had broken up their lives.

The people of Johnstown have never put up a marker at the dam site. They don't need anything to remind them of that thundering black day when the dam wall burst open and spilled death on the valley.

BIBLIOGRAPHY

BOOKS

Beale, Reverend David: *Through the Johnstown Flood*. Philadelphia, 1890.

Chapman, Reverend H. L.: *Memoirs of an Itinerant*. Privately published.

Connelly, Frank, and Jenks, George: *Official History of the Johnstown Flood*. Pittsburgh, 1889.

Dieck, Herman: *The Johnstown Flood*. Philadelphia, 1889.

Field, Reverend C. N.: *After the Flood*. Philadelphia, 1889.

Gramling, Oliver: *AP: The Story of News*. New York, 1940.

Greer, Margaret: *From Trail Dust to Star Dust*. Johnstown, 1959.

Heiser, Victor: *An American Doctor's Odyssey*. New York, 1937.

Johnson, Willis Fletcher: *History of the Johnstown Flood*. Privately published.

McLaurin, J. J.: *The Story of Johnstown*. Harrisburg, 1889.

O'Connor, Richard: *Johnstown—The Day the Dam Broke*. J. B. Lippincott Co., Philadelphia.

Slattery, Gertrude Quinn: *Johnstown and Its Flood*. Wilkes-Barre, 1936.

Walker, James: *The Johnstown Horror*. Chicago, 1889.

Works Progress Administration: *The Floods of Johnstown*. Johnstown, 1942.

MAGAZINES AND NEWSPAPERS

Harper's Weekly, June 8 and June 15, 1889.

Pennsylvania Magazine of History and Biography, Vol. 57. Philadelphia, 1933.

Western Pennsylvania Historical Magazine, Vol. 23. Pittsburgh, 1940.

New York: *Sun; Morning World; Tribune.*

Philadelphia: *Press; Public Ledger.*

Pittsburgh: *Commercial Gazette, Chronicle Telegraph.*

Johnstown: *Tribune.*

Index

Abbie, Aunt, 45, 67, 68
Adair, Alexander, 42, 43
Allegheny Mountains, 3, 5, 14
Allegheny River, 14, 151
Alma Hall, night in, 94-99, 116
Altoona, Penna., 142
American Doctor's Odyssey, 77
American House, 88
American Red Cross, 145, 146, 148, 163
American Steel and Iron Association, 20
Army engineers, 149
Associated Press (AP), 123-127

Babies, born during flood, 91
Barton, Clara, 145, 146
    quoted, 156, 157
    See also American Red Cross
Beale, The Reverend David (and family), 92-99, 117, 128
    as author of *Through the Johnstown Flood*, 94
    quoted, 116

Beaver, James A., Governor, 117, 135, 146, 148
Benford, Mr., 87, 88
Bethlehem Steel Corporation, 162
Bolivar, Penna., 111, 123, 124
Booth, Edwin, 149
Bowser sisters, 72, 119
Bravery, acts of, 54, 76, 77, 79-91, 100-108, 110-121
Brinker, Mr., 74, 75
Brinker, Mrs., 31, 32, 73-75
Brotherhood of Carpenters and Mechanics, 149
Bryan, Bessie, 52, 53
Buffalo Bill, 149
Buttermilk Falls, 5

Cambria City, Penna., 22, 32, 35, 42, 108, 112
Cambria Clubhouse, 103
Cambria County, Penna.
    Coroner's inquest in, 157
Cambria Iron Works, 20, 22, 23, 36, 41, 144
    after the flood, 135, 154
    and the flood, 32-35, 50, 62, 108, 114
    bought up by Bethlehem

Steel, 162
expansion of, 17
founding of, 16
workers' conditions at, 17
Carnegie, Andrew, 20, 22
Carnegie-Schwab-Frick steel combine, 17
Casualties, 129, 153
Central Telephone Office, 37-39
Chapman, The Reverend Henry, 4, 5, 30-32, 35, 73-75, 129, 150
Nellie, 31, 73-76
Chicago-New York Limited, 49
Children's Aid Society, 153
Citizens' Committee, 133
Citizens' Relief Headquarters, 129, 138
Civil War, 16, 40, 79
Clark, Rose, 101
Clement's Hotel, 163
Cokesville, 113
Communication, *see* Central Telephone Office, Western Union
Conemaugh, Penna., 29, 33, 34, 65
Conemaugh Borough, 22, 60, 72, 90
Conemaugh River, 14, 21, 38, 124
Conemaugh Valley, 5, 12
Connolly, Colonel, 123-127

Daisytown, Penna., survives flood, 116, 117
Dam, the Conemaugh Lake, 5-7, 18, 48-65
building of, 12, 13, 15, 16
bursts, 48-65
in danger, 27-29, 42
inspected, 21, 22
need for repair, 6, 7, 17, 18, 20-24, 157
today, 163, 164. *See also* Flood Control Act of 1936
Davis, Richard Harding, 137, 138
Deckert, Agent, 37
Dibert, John, 84
Duncan, Elvie, 76
Dougherty, Operator, 27-29, 49, 51
Dynamiting, and flood control, 150, 151

East Conemaugh, Penna., 22, 29, 34, 42, 51, 52, 61, 126, 156
Ebensburg, Penna., 126
Elder, Cyrus, 33-35, 154
Emma, Miss, 27, 28
Erie, Penna., 128
Evans, Burgess (Mayor), 61
Eyre, Richard, 42, 43

Fenn, Mrs., 133, 134, 149
Fire, at Stone Bridge, 100-109
First National Bank, 132
Fisher, George, 48, 49
Flood Control Act of 1936, 163
Flooding, described, 25, 26, 38, 53-57, 62, 63, 67, 68, 88, 112-114
and fire, 100-109
and legislation, 163
and relief operations, 142-159

and rescue operations, 110-121
recent, 162, 163
Foster, Barbara (and family), 119
Frick, Henry C., 20, 22
Fritz Hotel, 89
Fronheiser, John (and family), 102, 103
Fulton, John, 20, 98
family of, 98
reports dangers in dam, 21, 23

Gautier Wire Works, 32-34, 60, 72, 101, 114, 135
Gibbs, George
describes fire, 106, 107
describes flood, 38, 113, 114
describes state rule, 148
Green Hill, 43, 66, 119

Harrisburg, Penna., 29, 117, 125, 133
Harrisburg *Telegraph*, 138
Harrison, Benjamin, President, 44
Hart, Alec, Captain, 94, 95, 98, 117
Hartley, Mr., describes flood, 88
Hastings, Adjutant General, 133, 135, 136, 145, 146, 148, 155, 156
Heiser, Mr., 78-80
Heiser, Victor, 77, 79, 82, 83, 129
quoted, 78, 80
Hess, Engineer, 51, 52, 54, 56, 57

Hessler, Edward, 111
describes flood, 112
Horne, Joseph, 20
Housing problems, 154, 155
Hulbert House, 86, 87

Iron and steel industry, in Johnstown area, 6
ethnic origins of workers, 6
growth of, 16
start of, 13

Johns, Joseph, 12, 13
Johnstown, Penna.
and damage to churches, 73
description of, 4
flood hits, 66-78
founding of, 12
free from floods, 163, 164
immigration to, 12, 13
industry in, 13, 16, 17
lake and dam near, 5-7, 12-18, 20-24
population in 1930, 162
rainfall around, 4-6, 14, 24-26, 30, 161, 163
and rivers, 14
survivors of flood in, 79-99
and transportation, 13, 16
under state rule, 148
Johnstown flood, the
and the bursting dam, 48-65
and fire, 100-109
and struggle to survive, 79-99. *See also* Bravery, acts of
casualties from, 129, 153
help for survivors, 142-159
in full force, 66-78

newspaper coverage of, 3,
  122-141
rainfall and, 4-6, 24-26, 30
rebuilding after, 155, 156
responsibility for, 157
warning signs of, 12-29
Johnstown *Tribune*, 7, 37, 38,
  106, 113, 148, 156
  editorial in, 158

Keystone Hotel, 89
Kirk, Arthur, 150, 151
Klein, Mr., 89
Koch, Mr., 71
Krebs, Frederick, 32, 33, 72,
  73

Ladies' Relief Corps, 5
Lake Conemaugh, 18
Lamb, George, 49
Little Conemaugh River, 4, 14,
  22, 36, 85, 109, 151

Mangus, Mrs., 89
Masterton, Leudie, Mrs., 90
Matthews, Dr., 95, 98, 99, 144
McAchren, Max, 70, 71
McLaurin, John, 138
Mellon, Andrew, 20
Memorial Day Parade, 5, 9-11
Merchants Hotel, 89
Metz, Mrs., 71
Miller, Robert, describes flood,
  62
Millville, Penna., 34, 43, 108
Mineral Point, 27, 28, 34, 50,
  51, 140
Monongahela River, 14
Morrell, Dan, 20-23

Moxham, Tom, 117
Muddy Run, 25
Mussante, Mr., fruit dealer, 82

New Florence, Penna., 123
New York *Herald*, 139
New York *Sun*, 150
New York *Times*, 62
  quoted, 135-137
New York *World*, 158
Newspaper coverage, 3, 122-
  141

Ogle, Hetty, 40-42
  death of, 153
Ogle, Minnie, 41
"Oklahomas" (prefabricated
  houses), 155
O'Neil, Burgess (Mayor), 43
  and death of wife and baby,
  108
Orr, Harry, 123-125

Parke, John, Jr., 25-29, 48, 49
Paulson, Jennie, 52, 53
Pennsylvania Railroad, 16, 22,
  26, 34, 37, 43, 122, 124, 143,
  156
Philadelphia, Penna., 13, 52,
  126, 132, 146, 148, 158
Phillips, Major, 151
Phipps, Charles, describes flood,
  107-108
Pickerill, William, 27-29, 51
Pitcairn, Robert, 122
Pittsburgh, Penna., 3, 7, 13, 14,
  17-20, 22, 42, 52, 124-128,
  142, 143, 148-151, 158
Pittsburgh *Commercial Gazette*,
  25, 122, 123, 134

Pittsburgh Relief Committee, 143

Prospect, Penna., 108

Prospect Hill, 87, 145

Queen Victoria, 149

Quinn, Gertrude, 43-47, 66, 69-72, 118-121, 154
    describes flood, 67, 68

Quinn, James, 44-47, 66, 67, 119, 120

Quinn, Marie, 46, 47, 67

Quinn, Vincent, 44-47, 72, 120

Railroad disasters, 49-60

Rainfall, 4-6, 14, 24-26, 30, 161, 163

Rebuilding operations, 155, 156

Relief operations, 142-159

Rescue operations, *see* Bravery, acts of

Richwood, Charles, 59, 61
    describes flood, 57, 60

Richwood, Edith, 57, 59-61

Robinson, Dr., describes flood, 56

Ronesen, Michael, 77

Rose, Horace, Jr., 85

Rose, Horace, Mayor, 35-37, 83-85, 160, 161, 163

Rose, Percy, 84, 85

Rose, Winter, 84, 85

Ross family, 30, 31, 35

Ruff, Benjamin, 18, 21, 22

Sang Hollow, 110, 111, 122

Sanitation Corps, 144, 150

Schreder, William, describes flood, 53, 54

Schultz, Mrs., 107, 136

Sherman, William Tecumseh, General, 148

Sisters of Charity, 145

Skinner, George, 71

Smith, Joseph, 86, 87

Smith, William, 126, 127

South Fork, 5, 22, 23, 25, 27-29, 34, 37, 48, 49, 51, 158

South Fork Hunting and Fishing Club, 143, 157
    as owners of lake and dam, 7, 18
    attacked by newspapers, 134, 135, 158
    founding of, 18
    refuses to repair dam, 22

South Fork Run, 13, 24, 25

Stackhouse, Powell, 34

St. John's Church, 85, 104, 107, 145

Stone Bridge, 43, 66, 70, 71, 77, 83, 128, 140, 150-152
    fire at, 99, 100-109

Stony Creek, 4, 36, 66, 83, 85, 151

Swan, Dr., 85

Swank, George, 37

Tice, William, describes fire, 103, 104

Tittle, Dix (and family), 39, 40

Traut, Frank, 98

Trautwein, Father, describes fire, 104, 106

Typhoid danger, 144, 152

Unger, Colonel Elias, 23, 24, 26, 48, 158

Unique Skating Rink, 85
United States Government Signal Service, 5

Veterans' Hall, 5

Walters, James, 95, 96

Webber, Herb, 23, 24, 29
Western Union, 34, 38-41, 125-127, 153
Wetmore, 123-125
Wilson, J. P., 28
Woodvale, Penna., 22, 34, 61, 62, 64, 65, 114
World War I, 162

ABOUT THE AUTHOR

Hildegarde Dolson's books have been delighting readers for many years. Among the well-known titles are *We Shook the Family Tree, Guess Whose Hair I'm Wearing, The Great Oildorado*, which tells of America's first oil rush, and *William Penn*, a Landmark biography of the famous Quaker who founded Pennsylvania. In *Disaster at Johnstown*, Miss Dolson returns to the history of her native state.

Hildegarde Dolson started writing at the age of nine in Franklin, Pennsylvania. She now lives in Greenwich Village, in New York City, and spends her spare time painting and writing song lyrics.

ABOUT THE ILLUSTRATOR

Joseph Cellini was born in Hungary and studied at the Academy of Fine Arts in Budapest. Following the Hungarian revolt of 1956, he came to the United States with his wife, Eva, who is also an artist. They now live in Leonia, New Jersey, and have recently added a huge studio-workroom to their house.

Since his arrival in America, Mr. Cellini has been extremely busy with book and magazine illustration. For Random House he has illustrated a World Landmark, *Julius Caesar*, and with his wife he provided the drawings for *All About Engines and Power*.